Blockchains for Entrepreneurs

Simple Language, Code-free, Practical Ideas

Cut the Tech, Keep the Essentials

Your Clear, Concise, and Comprehensive Blockchain Guide

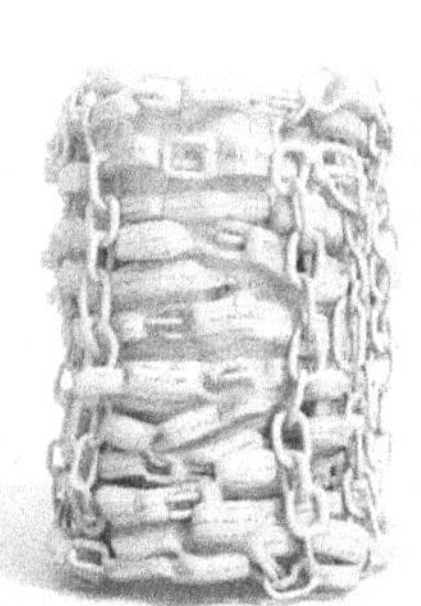

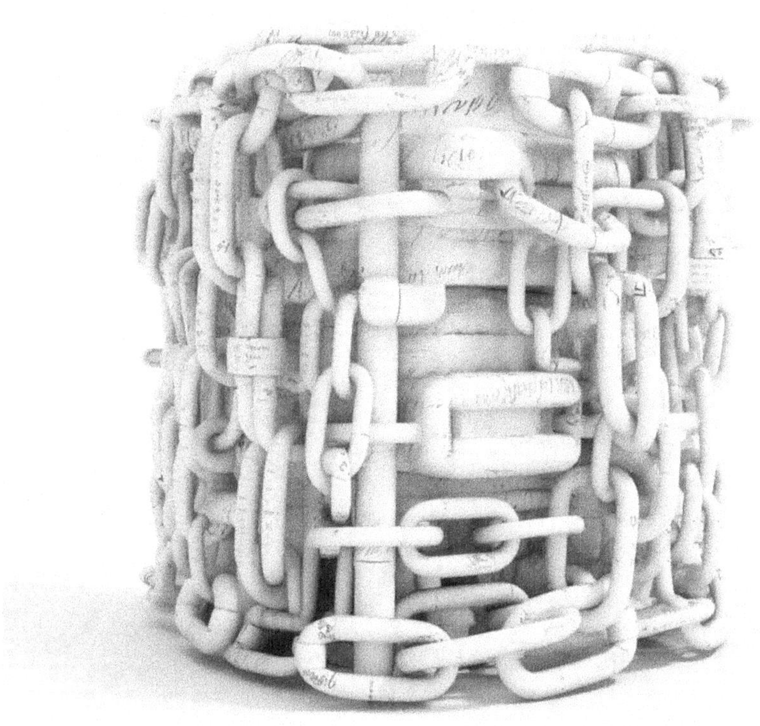

By Alex Rass

Published by ITBS LLC

www.itbsllc.com

First Edition

Table of Contents

Acknowledgements

As I embark on the journey of presenting this book, it's essential to pause and acknowledge the myriad of influences and support systems that have been instrumental in its creation. First and foremost, my deepest gratitude goes to my family, whose unwavering belief in my vision has been the cornerstone of my perseverance.

A special thanks to my friends, both within and outside the tech community, for their invaluable insights and mentorship. Their diverse perspectives have not only enriched this work but have also been a constant source of inspiration and motivation in my life. Ash Bennington, Lawrence Lewitinn, John Mendez, Serge and Jane Pustelnik, and many more.

And finally, to you, the reader, for embarking on this journey with me. This book is not just a reflection of my exploration into the world of blockchain and startups, but is also a testament to the collective curiosity and drive that propel this revolutionary technology forward. It is my sincere hope that the pages that follow will not only inform but also inspire you to delve deeper into the transformative potential of technology.

With heartfelt gratitude,

- Alex Rass.

In the fast-paced world of digital advancements, this technology isn't just a sidenote. It's creating a new specialty in business and in computer science, causing businesses to rethink their old ways and reinvent themselves. The technology leading this profound transformation? Blockchain. This groundbreaking innovation goes far beyond the realm of cryptocurrency. It's already started to disrupt industries and change the way we think about business operations, data security, transparency, and trust.

Now is the time to understand this technology, embrace it, and leverage its potential—not tomorrow, not next year, but right now. We are standing on the precipice of a revolution as significant as the advent of the internet itself. Blockchain technology presents a paradigm shift in how we organize and orchestrate economic, social, and even political systems. Like the internet, it is transformational, promising unprecedented possibilities for organizations willing to understand and harness its power.

But why the urgency? The answer is simple. Blockchain technology is rapidly maturing, and businesses worldwide are integrating it into their operations, yielding increased efficiency, security, and transparency. If you delay understanding and adopting blockchain, you risk being left behind in a world where your competitors are surging ahead. The longer you wait, the larger the gap becomes, and the harder it is to close.

This book serves as your guide to understanding what blockchain is, why it matters, and how it can revolutionize your business. It presents the concept in a non-technical, easy-to-grasp manner, designed to arm you with the knowledge you need to make informed decisions about implementing blockchain technology in your organization.

Despite being around for over a decade, blockchain is still in its infancy in terms of adoption and application, akin to the early days of the internet. It's a technology that, until recently, had been waiting for its moment, its tipping point. Now, we're witnessing that moment unfold. We're beginning to see the pieces fall into place, with improved infrastructure, growing regulatory clarity, increasing public awareness, and advancements in complementary technologies.

The surprising fact is that, unlike other established technologies, there are still very few juggernauts in the blockchain space. This presents a unique and unprecedented opportunity. The field is wide open, and the chances to become a first mover or an early adopter are still available for those daring enough to seize them.

As blockchain technology matures and becomes more mainstream, it's paving the way for wide adoption and limitless applications that extend far beyond its initial use in digital currencies. Today, we have the tools, the knowledge, and the frameworks needed to integrate blockchain into our business models and processes. We're on the brink of a mass adoption phase where blockchain will move from a fringe technology to a standard and expected solution across industries.

This nascent stage of development and its vast potential are what make the present moment so crucial. Now is the time to act, to learn, to adapt, and to be part of shaping the blockchain landscape. It's not just about keeping up with the competition—it's about pushing boundaries, breaking new ground, and ushering in the future.

Who Is This Book for?

If you're a C-level executive, entrepreneur, or anyone looking to understand how blockchain can be useful—without getting bogged down in technical jargon—this book is for you.

This book can also be used as course material for any level class, as it covers a full range of features to a sufficient degree for most classes.

There's no code, difficult lingo or buzzwords. Lots of "rocket science" level cryptography and math are used to develop blockchains. But it's irrelevant to putting these concepts to work as a business leader, so we will stick to human-friendly language.

With apologies to 95% of you, there will not be any trading advice or coin picks.

The book aims to provide a high-level understanding of blockchain technology and its implications for people and organizations. It focuses on strategic decision-making and the broader business implications rather than technical details, implementation or chain specifics. I hope this book will inspire revelations in even the most tech-averse among you on how this newfangled blockchain stuff can benefit your projects—new and old.

Books vs. Articles

You might ask: Why read a book on blockchains when you can just Google it?

When diving into a new topic, picking up a book can often be a more beneficial starting point than merely typing your queries into a search engine. This book is carefully curated and structured by an expert in the field, ensuring that the content is not only accurate but also comprehensive and logically organized.

In contrast, online searches might give you quick answers, but they often provide a narrow view, focusing on specific queries instead of offering an overarching perspective. They can also lead to a fragmented learning experience, with information scattered across different sources of varying credibility. This book will enable you to build a solid foundation of knowledge in far less time than an internet search.

Is This Guy Qualified to Give Me Advice?

No! But I have picked up a few things here and there.

I developed the world's first T0 on-chain settlement solution for an exchange, and later, the world's first decentralized Web3 crypto fintech lending solution. I have worked on a number of Web3 and nonfungible token (NFT) sites. I advise staffers at CoinDesk and RealVision on blockchain technology, have appeared in a documentary about blockchains and have published articles on real-life applications of cryptography and blockchain. I hold a graduate degree in computer science from one of the top institutions in the U.S. and have worked for top multinational investment banks and a management consulting firm.

Blockchain isn't the future; it's the present. The sooner you recognize its potential, the better equipped you'll be to navigate the exciting new world it's shaping. It's time to understand, adapt, and take control of this extraordinary opportunity. The blockchain revolution is happening right now, and it waits for no one. Your journey starts here. Let's dive in.

Disclaimer

This book provides general information on creating a business in the cryptocurrency sector and is intended for educational purposes only. It does not offer legal, financial, or professional advice. The cryptocurrency landscape is rapidly evolving, and laws and regulations vary significantly by jurisdiction. The author makes no representations or warranties regarding the accuracy, reliability, or completeness of the content provided.

Readers are advised to conduct their own due diligence and consult with professional advisors familiar with their specific situation for legal or financial advice. The author disclaims any liability for actions taken or not taken based on the content of this book. Engaging in cryptocurrency activities without adhering to the applicable laws and regulations can result in significant legal consequences.

By using this book, you acknowledge and agree that the information provided does not constitute legal or financial advice and that you will not rely on it as such. The author will not be liable for any losses or damages arising from your use of this book or the information contained within it.

Chapter 1. What Is a Blockchain?

In order to discuss the topic, we need to introduce the basics. Skip subsections if you already know this stuff.

- What is a blockchain?

- How does blockchain differ from traditional databases?

- Benefits and potential applications of blockchain technology.

- The origins of blockchain, its basic principles, and its key features, like decentralization, security, and transparency.

The simplest way to understand a blockchain is to think of it as a database.

What Is a Database?

A database is a bit like a digital library, but instead of books, it stores various types of information, such as text, numbers, and images. This information is organized in a structured way that makes it easy to find exactly what you need when you need it. Imagine if all the books in a library were just piled up in a big heap. It would be pretty difficult to find the book you wanted, right? In a database, just like in a well-organized library, everything has its place.

When we talk about a database, we often refer to two main parts: the data itself, and the way that data is structured or organized. The data might include all sorts of things, from the names and addresses of everyone in a town to the complete inventory of a store, or even the scores of every player in a video game.

The way the data is organized is also crucial. In many databases, data is stored in *tables*. You can think of these tables a bit like the Excel grid or like a grid of a chessboard, with rows and columns. Each row represents a single *record*—for example, one person's name and address, one item in a store's inventory, or one player's game scores. Each column represents a specific type of information, like last names, product prices, or highest scores.

The great thing about a database is that it doesn't just store information; it also makes it easy to manage that information. You can add new records, change existing records, or remove records that you no longer need. You can search through all the data to find exactly what you're looking for, sort the data in different ways, or even ask the database to answer questions like "Who has the highest score?" or "How many red sweaters do we have in stock?"

In all sorts of situations, from running websites to managing business information, databases play a key role. They help keep our information safe, organized, and easy to use—which is why understanding how they work is so valuable.

We can interface with them directly using dedicated tools that can display grids and let us build more and more complicated questions. Or we can connect to them through an application programming interface (API) and remotely request answers and send new data to be stored.

The takeaway: A database is a digital system that stores, organizes, and manages information. It arranges data in a structured way, making it easy to add, change, remove, search, sort, and analyze the data. And it can be accessed locally or remotely.

How Is a Blockchain Like a Database?

A blockchain can store the data you want in a structured way. Blockchains store data across all available or participating nodes for redundancy and security. What is stored can not be modified or deleted.

Some blockchains, like Ethereum, can also run code on the *server side* (that's what miners do) to modify state and data.

As with any technology layer, new databases are designed to do certain things better than existing databases.

For blockchains, these tasks include handling of data in a way that is transparent to the users so old transactions can be verified, performing accounting tasks easily, managing ownership of a resource, and more.

Databases are usually centralized. They can't modify data without a central node (or have similar bottlenecks). Blockchains, in contrast, are decentralized and rely on complex mathematics to ensure that the entire system can go on working and existing without reliance on individual nodes, people, or systems.

Unlike a typical database, a blockchain can function across firewalls, regions and networks of all types—this is called cross-network interoperability. "Distributed" doesn't begin to describe it.

But these benefits don't come without compromises:

- Blockchains are slower than other databases.

- New forms of security attacks (depending on encryption used) can compromise the whole thing.

- The cost of storing information (data/code) can be exorbitant compared to other methods.

Basic Working Principles

A blockchain, at its core, is a sequentially ordered list of changes to some initial state.

We take a state of X and we add increments. "Move amount1 money from account1 to account2." "Add a chunk of data under this account." "Call this method/function in this code and pass these parameters. Record the resulting state (or error) here." And so on.

Software is used to sum up all these changes into a "current state" where money has all been moved, transactions of all kinds have succeeded and failed and now we know who has what and all the variables are set.

Then a new block comes in and the "current" state gets updated, with slight delays for remote or slower nodes.

(Block)Chain Logistics

As blockchain code is extremely complicated and expensive to write and maintain, projects and companies will typically reuse the code from an existing blockchain. But aside from which code to run, how does a blockchain come to be?

One or more people or companies come together and agree on the following:

- Who will own/govern the new chain.
  This could be a group of individuals or companies.

- Who will run the nodes (think *tiny servers*).
  This can be "people of the world" (public), "guys in suits behind server room doors" (private), or a combination (consortium).
  For example: Ethereum is public, a bank can run an internal blockchain (private), a food bank can run their own, with read-only nodes for anyone who wants to connect (consortium).

- Who will compute the new state of the chain.
  This, like node ownership, could be anyone with the rights to add records (blocks). Many chains' *miners* are paid to process incoming records and record the new state.

- Which algorithm (called consensus mechanisms) to use for maintaining records/blocks.
  This is largely a point for cryptographic nerds, but popular choices include *proof of work,*

proof of stake and *proof of authority*. It's a hot research topic and new ones are proposed on a regular basis. They determine how the writer for the next block is chosen in a way that keeps the chain secure and valid. This has a lot of security vs speed vs scalability implications for the chain and should be chosen with care. The details of these algorithms are beyond the scope of this book, but are easily found through search.

- Self-hosted vs professionally hosted.
  Amazon and others are now in the business of running chains for others. I suspect this will become a huge business, in time. If you are hosting yourself - there are a lot of technical issues to deal with. But if you simply have a node to a chain hosted professionally - things will likely work smoother and be more secure for smaller chains.

- Will the platform have underlying currency?
  (e.g., bitcoin or ether)

- Will user-supplied code be allowed on the chain?

A company may bring up MySQL (a popular relational database) for internal use and then decide to also bring up a blockchain for internal use. And none of us will ever have access to either. Or they may choose to open up access directly, through nodes, or indirectly, through a website/API.

We can make many regular databases distributed by running more nodes (servers). We can also make blockchain distributed by giving it more nodes. Its main purpose is to be distributed—but it doesn't have to be.

See? All "databases" follow similar patterns.

To read from a chain, one usually has to run the node software (most blockchains give away their source code) and make API requests to it for data. Alternatively, one can play caching games (record all data into a cache as it comes in and read that) or make requests from others who run nodes.

To write to a chain, one submits the changes in a form:

- Monetary transaction
  (Pay address 0x123 some platform money)

- Code submission
  (Upload my new code so I can use it later)

- Function calls to someone's code
  (Go to address 0x123 and call a method foo() with these parameters)

Once the change is submitted, the chains that use miners will wait for one to integrate the change into the new *block*, which is appended to the chain.

Most current blockchains use miners.

These are people who expend resources (time, money, computing equipment, electricity) to ensure chains run smoothly. They monitor incoming requests and, when given a chance by the chain's protocols, will aggregate multiple updates into one block and add it to the chain.

Miners are typically paid by the chain or by its users. Reward systems can be wildly different between chains, limited only by the imagination of the creators. Communication protocols, encryption, and the frequency and amount of payment to miners are only some of the things that can be different between blockchains.

Many people mistakenly think they can simply jump into mining and make money. Most of these folks will be learning some hard lessons, including why mining doesn't work as a small-scale business.

Professional mining firms usually find sources of cheap energy and market makers to handle the coin they earn. They're located in giant data centers designed to handle the mining equipment dedicated to processing specific chains.

Everyone else gets bought out by them, if they are lucky enough to not run out of money and close first.

On-chain, Off-chain and Side-chain

Any specific blockchain will come with conditions set by the combination of rules and costs dictated by the governing authority and the choices they've made to date.

Not all blockchains are created equal. Cost and speed, in transactions per second, are of major concern.

In years past, there have been periods when Ethereum transaction fees, called gas fees, spiked significantly—up to $50 per transaction. There was a surge in the use of Ethereum due to the growing popularity of decentralized finance (DeFi) applications and non-fungible tokens (NFTs), among other factors.

This typically happens when the Ethereum network is congested with many pending transactions. The more users are transacting on the network, the higher the demand for computational power, and consequently, the higher the fees.

This is due to the auction-style mechanism Ethereum uses for transactions, where users bid (gas prices) to have their transactions included in the blockchain. Some months the network was simply overwhelmed by the number of transactions that users were trying to process. This has been fixed, but at the time it created uncertainty and a strong demand for alternative solutions. Entire projects were delayed or moved off Ethereum because of this.

These concerns gave rise to *off-chain* and *side-chain* transactions.

In an off-chain transaction, your system will only store summaries or key transactions on the main chain. Irrelevant or numerous transactions are processed either in an entirely different manner—off-chain—or on a side chain with faster or cheaper transactions, engineered to connect to your main chain.

Off-chain transactions create issues with transparency. Side chains, for their part, have proven to be difficult to implement, hard to use, and plagued with technical problems that have resulted in loss of assets. Search for Polygon to learn more or go to https://polygon.technology.

These are not to be confused with fully alternative chains, where a transaction is moved off of your main chain to another chain completely.

Pretty Good Privacy (PGP)

Imagine you want to send a secret message to your friend, but you're afraid someone might intercept it and read it. What do you do? This is where PGP—Pretty Good Privacy—comes in.

PGP is like a special coded language that only you and your friend understand. When you want to send a message to your friend, you use this special language (we call this *encrypting* the message) to transform your message into something that looks like gibberish to everyone else. Only your friend, who knows the code, can transform it back to the original message (we call this *decrypting* the message). Think how spies would communicate with one another.

In practice: Think of PGP as a black box that takes two keys to operate. The *public key* is safe to distribute and goes to everyone you talk to. The *private key* is for safekeeping. When you send a message through this black box, you pass in your public key and that of your destination party. When you want to decode a message from a third party, you pass in your private key and their public key, and their message is decrypted.

The same PGP black box has another cool feature you can use to authenticate your message without encrypting it, with a "signature." It's like a digital version of your handwritten signature, helping your readers confirm that the message indeed came from you and wasn't tampered with along the way. You run your message through the PGP black box, but request to get a signature instead of an encrypted message and out comes a line of weird text. This text fed into a black box along with your public key will allow any reader to verify that the message indeed came from you. That signature, often labeled as a "PGP signature," is often put on files and messages to verify the authenticity of the file or message.

In a nutshell, PGP helps keep your messages private and verifies they're genuinely from you, with an unforgeable digital signature.

This mechanism is used heavily throughout blockchain technology to authenticate and verify. This is how you can send commands that control your account to miners and they can read and obey instructions knowing they definitely came from you.

This is covered in greater detail later in the book.

Key Management

One of the biggest issues in cryptography is how to manage private keys. If your private key is compromised, someone could empty your account. If you lose your key, you lose your assets.

Your assets are also gone if you deposit all your crypto at a trading firm and that firm goes bust, hence the expression "not your keys, not your coin."

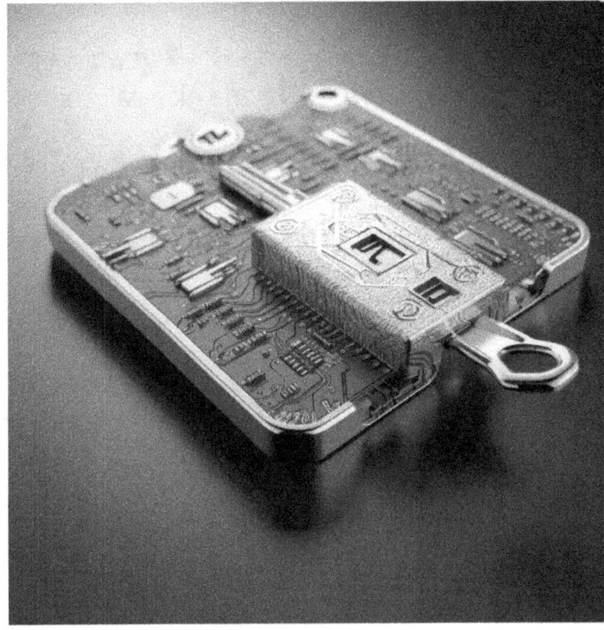

Popular methods of key management include zip drives (some come with a combination lock for protection), a piece of paper shoved under a mattress (literal or metaphorical), and digital and physical wallets.

Wallets

What is a wallet? Different blockchains use the same word to describe a number of different things.

Let's clear this up.

A *digital wallet* is a software-based system that securely stores users' payment information and passwords for payment methods and websites. It can also hold digital assets like cryptocurrencies, loyalty rewards, and digital identification cards. By using a digital wallet, users can complete purchases easily and quickly, often through contactless transactions, and manage their assets across various platforms.

How is this accomplished:

Each user has one or more addresses on the chain. Sometimes many. Don't think of your address as just an account at your bank—think of it as a safety deposit box at your bank. You can put all kinds of things in it, and only you have access.

Your favorite app store may have *wallet software* (or a *software wallet*) supporting a specific blockchain. If the software supports the chain you are trying to use, it will know to "generate an address" there and how to keep track of the assets stored at that address.

You can usually generate as many addresses as you want, for free. Sometimes multiple wallet software programs are needed to store all your assets across different chains, as most wallet apps can only handle a few chains.

Typically, when the software generates an address, it calculates your private keys for that address. No one else will know them unless you share them or your wallet software does.

The job of the wallet software is to store your keys, but it is important to create a backup. Some wallets offer additional functionality, including uploading keys to their servers. Be skeptical as companies often get hacked. Making a backup will differ based on wallets used, but typically involves storing access keys somewhere safe. Look into USB drives with pin codes or similar specialty secure drives.

So now you have an address (or a few) on a chain, and you can start accumulating assets, code, and more. You can use third-party services to send assets to or from your address, run transactions against it, and do lots of cool stuff.

But it bears repeating: *If you lose your keys, you lose your funds.* Key management has been the biggest issue in cryptography since it started. So manage your keys with care.

Virtual Machines

Many of the newer generation chains support virtual machines (VMs): the ability to run code someone wrote and uploaded. This is the mechanism that allows chains to not only handle currencies, but also refine contracts around data and digital currencies, including defining digital currencies themselves.

This enables the creation of *smart contracts*—self-executing contracts with predefined terms and conditions written in code. They enable the automation of transactions, the establishment of trustless agreements, and the execution of complex logic on the blockchain.

Examples of this are:

- Legal contracts like escrow (a third party temporarily holds money for repayment of a debt).
- Gambling without oversight, borders or casinos.

This gives rise to *decentralized applications* (dApps) that run on the blockchain. They can leverage the capabilities of the VM to execute code and interact with the blockchain's smart contracts.

Not all blockchains support VMs. But some have a partially exposed VM, allowing owners to supply code that users can run.

How Cryptocurrencies Work

Now let's dive into how cryptocurrencies work, their significance, and the value they can bring to businesses.

Blockchains, with their inherent secure and decentralized nature, serve as the foundational structure for creating and managing digital assets. These assets often take the form of tokens, which can represent a variety of items. This could be cryptocurrencies like bitcoin or ether, utility tokens that provide access to a specific service, security tokens tied to equity or debt, or even tokens symbolizing ownership of a digital or physical asset like real estate or art.

In practical terms, these digital assets are created and managed using wallet addresses, which are uniquely linked to owners via cryptographic security measures. Essentially, these wallet addresses are like secure digital lockboxes. Numerical values are then associated with these addresses, signifying ownership. This could represent complete ownership or a certain percentage of an asset.

These digital assets can be designed with various functionalities. For example, they could permit transfers, allowing the owner to send or receive assets from another wallet. Depending on the asset's design, other features might include the ability to temporarily halt transfers or generate additional tokens, which is akin to printing more money.

For businesses, digital assets open new avenues for value exchange, investment, and asset management. They can democratize access to capital by enabling businesses to raise funds globally through token sales, rather than relying on traditional capital markets. They also create opportunities for tokenizing physical assets, making them more liquid, divisible, and easily transferable.

However, it's worth noting that managing digital assets comes with its own set of challenges, including regulatory compliance, security, and the technical complexity of blockchain technology. Businesses should take a thoughtful and informed approach when integrating digital assets into their operations.

NFTs vs. Digital Coins

In a nutshell, NFTs are unique digital items that can represent just about anything online. They're different from regular coins because each is one-of-a-kind and thus can't be swapped on a like-for-like basis.

You know how you can have a one-of-a-kind collectible card, like a rare baseball card, that's super valuable because there's no other exactly like it in the world? An NFT is the digital version of that, stored on a blockchain. NFTs can represent all sorts of things: digital art, virtual real estate in online worlds, even tweets.

Unlike dollars or bitcoins, where each unit is exactly the same, each NFT is unique. If you have a dollar and I have a dollar, we can swap those dollars, and it wouldn't matter because they're worth the same. That's what we call *fungible*. But NFTs are not interchangeable. It's like trading a rare baseball card for another one. They might both be baseball cards, but they're not the same, because one might be much more valuable or desired than the other.

How File Storage Works

Since blockchains are designed to be highly distributed, it's important to define rules such that users don't just upload garbage data and expect others to host it forever. Most blockchains punish data loads, increasing costs exponentially as the data size of a given submission increases.

This led to specially designed blockchain systems for file storage using various mechanisms to discourage frivolous uploads. They are governed by different rules and often designed to self-purge and reward node owners for storing data.

In the InterPlanetary File System (IPFS), files are not organized using traditional names or paths as seen in conventional storage systems. Instead, each file resides at a distinct address within the network. The presence or absence of data at a specific address is treated as binary—either it contains something or it doesn't. This approach enables effective deduplication of files and allows for more efficient retrieval.

For entrepreneurs considering IPFS, remember that as a decentralized system, it's both robust and resilient, but it also requires a thoughtful approach to data management. Understanding how to incentivize other nodes to store your data and maintaining your own nodes could be vital for success. Furthermore, consider potential privacy, security, and compliance issues that may arise, since once data is uploaded to IPFS, it's tough to completely remove.

Chain Data

These are the typical ways to read data on the blockchain:

1. The user runs their own node software (most secure, high complexity).
2. They use a 3rd party service that runs node software and offers an API (less secure, low complexity).

There are a number of companies you can call on to fetch data from a chain, usually at a cost for the convenience. While these services don't support all chains, are inflexible in how they fetch your data, and can pose a security risk, they are nonetheless very popular. Running one's own node is a fairly taxing proposition as it requires fast network connectivity and processing power to constantly update the state of the chain. A lot of wallet management software and Web3 sites use these third-party services to request data from blockchains and issue commands to the chains.

Web3 and How It (Kinda) Works

Having all these pieces in place allows us to do the unthinkable: create a website that runs not on a typical server or a cluster but on a distributed blockchain. We've arrived at the world of Web3: bottlenecks gone, infinite uptime guaranteed, magical unicorns flying by. Right?

In reality, it's not that simple. Most Web3 sites come with terrible bottlenecks, often worse than traditional Web2 servers. So let's work it out step by step.

The typical Web3 site skeleton today looks like this:

1. Page sources (your HTML, CSS, font files and so on) are stored in IPFS (file blockchain).
   To store them, we run a server that seeds the IPFS chain with our files.

   We could store ALL the files in IPFS on the blockchain, but most projects, out of laziness, deposit all static documents and configuration files on a web server.

2. Pages are written with heavy JavaScript to allow interactions between the page and an in-browser enabled wallet software. This allows the site to do authentication as well as digital transactions.
3. Whenever a page needs access to data stored on a blockchain, it either needs to go back to a hosted server for it or rely on your software wallet for data.

The core issues with Web3 are as follows:

1. IPFS itself is great, but a typical Web3 implementation relies heavily on traditionally hosted services.
2. Running a Web2 server is a violation of the "distributed" and "no bottleneck" approach as that server can be taken down easily through the Domain Name System (DNS) or by other means.
3. These implementations are specific to the wallet software installed.
4. Going to third-party services or the company's own hosting to fetch on-chain data negates the "distributed" benefit, making it no better than Web2.

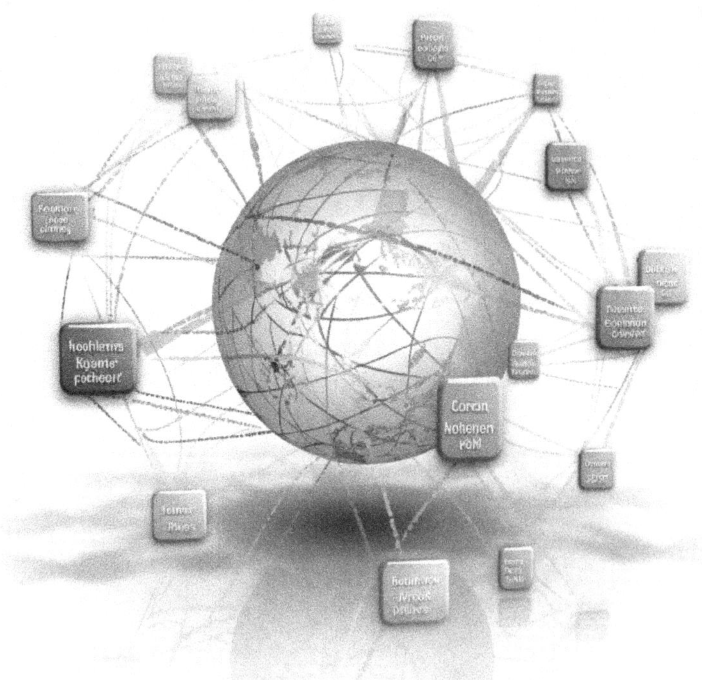

There are ways to architect around these issues and create a truly distributed system, but it becomes hard for the general public to use. Some wallets are trying to address this, but so far it's a work in progress.

We can hope that Web4 will come along and solve all these problems. But for now, don't panic. Use any pieces of Web3 and Web2 that you like. The most important part is to satisfy your business requirements. Not every solution needs all the bells and whistles.

Chapter 2. What Is Blockchain For?

This chapter is why this book was written: to show off practical use cases and advantages of adding blockchains and their overhead to projects. Blockchain can bring significant value and disrupt existing business models. Here's how.

Key Benefits

1. **Identification:** Blockchain technology is highly effective in verifying and protecting digital identities. Through the use of cryptographic techniques and digital signatures, the identity of parties involved in a blockchain transaction can be authenticated with high accuracy. It reduces the risk of identity theft, fraud, and unauthorized activity. For example, in a supply chain, each product or component could have a unique, verifiable identity on the blockchain, ensuring authenticity.
2. **Transparency:** Blockchains are inherently transparent due to their distributed nature. All transactions are visible to all nodes on the network, making the entire system highly transparent and traceable. This is especially valuable in scenarios where tracking the origin, authenticity, or compliance of products is important. For instance, a consumer could trace the origins of a product all the way back to its raw materials, or auditors could easily trace financial transactions to ensure compliance.
3. **Anonymity:** Blockchains can provide a level of anonymity because they use unique codes called cryptographic keys instead of personal information to identify users. When you send a transaction on a blockchain, it doesn't show your name or your physical address, just your digital "address," which is a string of numbers and letters. It's like sending a letter using a secret code name instead of your real name. Even though all the transactions are recorded on the blockchain and can be seen by anyone, they won't know it's you unless they can link your digital address to your real-world identity.
4. **Security:** Transactions on a blockchain are highly secure. They are linked to previous transactions, and any alteration of a transaction would require the alteration of all subsequent transactions, which is computationally impractical. Combined with the use of cryptographic techniques, this ensures that once data is recorded on the blockchain, it cannot be easily tampered with. This is particularly useful in sectors where data integrity is paramount, such as financial services, health care, or any form of record-keeping.
5. **Efficiency:** Blockchain can dramatically increase efficiency in several ways. By eliminating the need for intermediaries, transactions and processes can be carried out faster and more smoothly. Smart contracts automate complex processes and agreements, reducing the potential for errors and delays. The transparency of the blockchain also reduces the time required for reconciliation and dispute resolution. For example, in a supply chain context, a blockchain could provide real-time, trustworthy information about the location and status of goods, dramatically speeding up the process and reducing the risk of errors or fraud.
6. **Immutability:** Once data is written into a blockchain, it is incredibly difficult to change or delete. This feature ensures the permanence and integrity of data, which is particularly beneficial in use cases such as record-keeping, contract validation, and tracking of goods in a supply chain.
7. **Decentralization:** The distributed nature of blockchain provides resilience against single points of failure, such as centralized servers that can be attacked or go down. In a

blockchain, each node has a copy of the entire blockchain, which makes the network significantly more resilient.

8. **Trustless Transactions:** Blockchain allows parties that do not trust each other to interact and transact in a secure and verifiable way without needing intermediaries. This can be particularly beneficial in peer-to-peer marketplaces, supply chain relationships, or any other transaction where trust is a concern.

9. **Automation and Smart Contracts:** Blockchain enables the use of smart contracts, which are self-executing contracts where the terms of the agreement are directly written into lines of code. These allow for a high degree of automation in processes, which can reduce the need for manual oversight and speed up transaction times.

10. **Cost Reduction:** By eliminating the need for intermediaries and reducing the risk of fraud, blockchain can lead to significant cost savings in various processes. This is particularly relevant in financial transactions and cross-border payments.

11. **Interoperability and Standardization:** Blockchain can act as a shared, universal infrastructure that enables greater interoperability between different systems and organizations. This can be particularly useful in fragmented industries like health care, where data interoperability is a significant challenge.

12. **Tokenization and Digital Assets:** Blockchain allows for the creation and management of digital assets, from cryptocurrencies to tokenized versions of physical assets. These digital assets can create new business models and revenue streams.

13. **Reality, via Oracles:** Introduced to provide external data to a closed storage and computational system, through a system of API interfaces

14. **Innovation and Competitive Advantage:** Implementing blockchain can be a source of competitive advantage, positioning the organization as an innovative leader in its field. It can also provide opportunities to develop new services or products based on the technology.

Let's look at each of these benefits in a bit more detail.

Identification

Identification is a fundamental step in any system, even in scenarios where users remain anonymous. Properly identifying a user typically involves implementing authentication mechanisms. Authentication verifies the user's identity through various methods such as passwords, biometrics, or tokens. Once a user is authenticated, the system can grant appropriate access privileges and personalize the user's experience. This crucial process not only ensures security but also paves the way for personalized and secure interactions within the system.

Through Cryptography

After some embarrassing and expensive security hacks, Google gave all employees time-based one-time password (TOTP) authentication and hasn't seen a significant breach through user credentials since 2009. TOTP, PGP, and similar technologies enhance the security of accounts within blockchain systems. Security matters. To see how it's achieved, let's examine PGP.

PGP is a large topic, so please research PGP elsewhere if you need higher detail. For book's purposes, we just need the broad concepts:

You generate a key pair (two keys) using an algorithm.

1 public + 1 private.

Your digital wallet will store both. The public key will be either shared with the world by some shared mechanism (some known and trusted public server) or, for blockchains where there is no trust, there will be an algorithm to calculate the keys and the address of the account. Do that and you get an account and the keys to it.

This provides us with some interesting abilities:

1) Sign clear-text messages to guarantee authenticity
2) Encrypt messages to hide content
3) Authenticate to third-party systems
4) Authenticate across services that do not share data among them nor have to trust one another

Cryptographic keys are available through blockchain libraries and generic security libraries available everywhere, for all platforms. Expect to see them in more places as the security flaws of typical usernames and passwords—and the annoyance of having to remember them—become ever more clear.

Here's an example of cryptographic authentication:

A user comes to a website. The website requests a digital wallet (Metamask, for example). The user uses the wallet to sign a message to the website. The website verifies the signature against the one on the blockchain. The site now recognizes that this user is the same as the user who owns the specified blockchain account.

The benefits of this method:

- Nothing is typed in, so one can steal a password by watching the keyboard activity.
- No Post-It notes under the keyboard with passwords.
- No need for third-party password storage services, which are prone to hacking.
- No phishing attacks would work as all requests are time-stamped and the signatures are specific to the request or requestor.

Through NFTs

Imagine you want to get into a super-exclusive online game or a real-life concert. They won't let just anyone in, right? You'd need a ticket or a pass of some sort. That's where NFTs can come in.

Let's say the people running the game or the concert decide to issue these passes as NFTs. Because an NFT is a unique digital item that's recorded on a blockchain, it's easy to verify who owns it. When you show up at the game or concert, they can check the blockchain to see if you really own the NFT pass.

NFTs can also be used on websites. Maybe there's a special part of a website that only certain people are allowed to access. The website could use NFTs as digital "keys" to this part of the site.

So, by using NFTs, venues and websites can make sure that only the people who are supposed to get in can get in. Because it's all recorded on a blockchain, it's difficult to cheat the system.

Because NFTs can be bought and sold, you could potentially sell your pass if you no longer need it. The exact functionality of the keys—including transferability, and whether or when they expire—can be controlled through the code behind the NFT, whenever the chain supports it.

NFT authentication has become a cottage industry in itself. Collab.Land, for example, created an entire business by enabling Telegram and Discord groups to require NFTs for entry.

Transparency

This is a biggie, since transparency is the biggest selling point for using blockchains.

A blockchain, at its core, is a sequentially ordered list of changes to an initial state.

Software is used to sum up all these changes into a "current state," but all the incremental blocks are all there, unchanged from the initial copy, and the full trail can be authenticated and verified. This guarantees that EvilCorp hasn't inserted any false records or deleted any records.

There is a way to add information that is encrypted and not visible to unauthorized observers. But all records are associated with an account and are therefore cryptographically linked to it. Those who can read the data can maintain transparency either through decryption or via "zero proof" mechanisms.

There is always a way for regular databases to mimic this immutability (inability to change) of records through, say, stored procedures or special table permissions. But anyone who hacks the database, or simply has higher access, can go into these tables and modify them—sometimes by mistake, sometimes by malice. And this happens a lot.

So by using a blockchain you can mathematically guarantee to your users, partners or VCs that the data you are storing inside the blockchain is secure, ordered, transparent to audit, and compliant with generally accepted accounting principles.

Data can still be manipulated if someone steals a particular private key, but the damage is limited to that account, and previous history can't be manipulated. So design systems with that in mind.

The transparency of blockchain can be a powerful feature, but it also requires careful handling of data to respect privacy and confidentiality. Any business considering using blockchain for transparency must also consider how to protect sensitive information.

Examples:

Accounting: Company A can put its accounting transactions into a blockchain to demonstrate books aren't being cooked and offer transparency into how money is being spent. A public or private blockchain can be used to restrict who sees the data.

Logs and Records: Company B has a need to make statements "on the record." If it logs its messages on a blockchain, with an account it claims as its own, Anyone can verify the date and content of these statements and know that they came from the company.

Take the street artist Banksy, who works anonymously and then claims his creations via Twitter. An employee, or anyone else, with access to his account can modify a time record or erase the post altogether. His posts are at risk of being flagged and removed by the system automatically, or his account could be shut down.

On a blockchain, he would not run these risks, as universal time and record are immutable. Every news agency could subscribe to changes to his account and be notified automatically when new artworks appear.

Tracking: Company C ships cabbage to stores from many vendors. They want to know where any container is at any time—and if a box is contaminated, where it came from. The company gives every container an ID (or an account) and then writes records against it each time it gets touched (warehouses, trucks, stores). Now anyone with understanding of this data can trace any problems all the way up the supply chain. The company now has a wealth of new metrics at its disposal—which truck drivers are slower, which stores to warn of a contamination source, which warehouses are less efficient at transfers, and so on.

Real Estate Transactions: A blockchain-based real estate platform could provide transparent, secure, and efficient property transactions. It could record and verify property deeds, facilitate transparent property sales, and even enable fractional property ownership.

Charitable Donations: A blockchain-based platform could bring transparency to charitable donations, letting donors see exactly where their money is going and how it's being used. This could help reduce fraud and administrative costs in the charity sector, and make people more confident in donating.

Healthcare Records Management: A blockchain-based system for managing healthcare records could provide a secure, transparent, and interoperable system for storing and sharing patient data. This could give patients greater control over their data, and make it easier for healthcare providers to coordinate care.

Voting Systems: A blockchain-based voting platform could provide a transparent and secure way to conduct elections, reducing the risk of fraud or tampering, and making the results verifiable by anyone.

Food Safety and Quality Control: A blockchain-based system could provide transparency for consumers about the origin and safety of their food. From farm to table, each step in the food's journey could be recorded on the blockchain, allowing consumers to verify its source, processing, and handling.

Environmental Sustainability: A blockchain-based platform could provide transparent tracking of carbon emissions and other environmental data. Companies could use this platform to demonstrate their sustainability efforts, and consumers could use it to make more informed purchasing decisions.

Education and Credential Verification: Schools and universities could issue degrees, certifications, and other credentials on a blockchain. This would allow anyone to easily verify the authenticity of these credentials, reducing the risk of fraud.

Art Authenticity and Provenance: An online marketplace using blockchain could track the ownership history and authenticity of artwork and collectibles. This transparency would help prevent fraud and forgery in the art market.

Anonymity

Anonymity Through Accounts

Blockchain is essentially a digital ledger of all transactions that have taken place within the system. Each transaction is recorded with the *digital addresses* of the sender and the receiver, along with the transaction amount. However, these digital addresses, also known as public keys, are not inherently linked to the identities of the users involved in the transaction.

The digital addresses are derived from cryptographic keys. Each user has a private key and a corresponding public key. The private key is kept secret by the user, while the public key is shared with the network and used to create the user's digital address. When a user makes a transaction, they sign it with their private key, and anyone in the network can verify the signature using the corresponding public key. This provides a level of security, as transactions cannot be tampered with without having the private key.

The use of cryptographic keys means that, on the surface, transactions do not reveal any personal information about the users involved. The digital addresses don't contain any personal data; they're just strings of numbers and letters. However, it's worth noting that the level of anonymity provided by a blockchain depends largely on how it's used.

In the case of bitcoin, for example, while the blockchain does not contain inherent personal identifiers, if a user's digital address can be linked to their real-world identity, their transactions can potentially be traced. This is often referred to as pseudonymity rather than full anonymity.

For those who seek greater anonymity, certain types of cryptocurrencies, known as privacy coins (like monero or zcash), use advanced cryptographic techniques to obscure the details of transactions, making it more difficult to trace transactions back to the users involved.

Users can take additional steps to preserve their privacy, such as using new addresses for each transaction, using privacy-enhancing software to obscure their internet connection, or using certain services that mix transactions together to make them harder to trace.

It's important to note that the anonymity of blockchain transactions can be misused for illegal activities. As such, it's a topic of ongoing debate and regulatory scrutiny, and the level of anonymity that can be achieved may change as regulations evolve.

While blockchain technology offers a significant level of anonymity through the use of cryptographic keys and digital addresses, the degree of anonymity can vary and is dependent on both the specific technology used and the user's behavior.

Remember, while blockchain can offer strong privacy features, any business working with anonymity needs to respect laws and regulations around financial transactions, privacy, and data protection. The goal should be to balance the benefits of anonymity with the need to prevent illegal activities.

Examples:

Privacy-Focused Payment Services: Given the increasing concerns around privacy, businesses could develop payment services that leverage privacy-focused cryptocurrencies like Monero or Zcash. These services could be used for legal, privacy-sensitive transactions, such as online purchases where the buyer prefers not to share their personal information.

Anonymous Digital Content Platforms: A blockchain-based platform could enable creators to publish content anonymously. This could be particularly beneficial for whistleblowers, investigative journalists, or authors in regions with strict censorship laws. Readers could tip their favorite authors with cryptocurrency to support their work. Think Twitter with the ability to bypass all firewalls and censorship controls.

Privacy-Oriented Web Services: With the rise in data breaches and surveillance, there's growing demand for privacy-centric web services. Blockchain technology could be used to develop anonymous web browsing tools, email services, or cloud storage solutions that don't track user data.

Digital Identity Verification: Businesses could leverage blockchain's anonymity to create digital identity systems. Users would be able to prove who they are without revealing unnecessary personal information. This could be used in online voting, age verification, or any other scenario where identity needs to be confirmed without revealing additional personal data. Could be used to replace the use of Social Security numbers as identifiers in the U.S.

Private Real EstateTransactions: Blockchain could facilitate anonymous real estate transactions, allowing parties to buy and sell property while maintaining their privacy. This could appeal to high-profile individuals who prefer to keep their property dealings private.

Anonymous Charity Platforms: A blockchain-based platform could allow individuals to make charitable donations anonymously, encouraging more people to donate by ensuring their privacy.

Private Ownership: A blockchain can have a roster of who owns what percent of a company or entity without naming the parties. The roster can be used for percent ownership or number of shares. The blockchain would allow account owners to receive earned royalties and vote on resolutions—all anonymously.

Anonymity Through Encryption

Now add the fact that records we store can be encrypted.

If you want to protect data—any kind of data—it can be made unreadable to everyone outside of trusted parties. Any encryption can be utilized, as you are not required to use the same encryption algorithms the chain itself uses.

While encrypting data on a blockchain can provide strong security benefits, it's also crucial to ensure the proper management of encryption keys. If a key is lost, the encrypted data may become irretrievable. Any business model based on blockchain encryption needs to have robust procedures for key management and recovery.

Examples:

Secure Document Storage and Verification: Companies could offer secure storage services for important documents like contracts, property deeds, or certificates. The documents would be encrypted and stored on a blockchain, ensuring they can't be tampered with and allowing anyone to verify their authenticity.

Health Data Management: A blockchain-based platform could securely store encrypted health data, such as medical records or genomic data. This would provide patients with control over their own data and allow it to be easily shared with healthcare providers in a secure and transparent manner. In addition, access to parts of the patient's data can be limited, far exceeding the level of security of most solutions today.

Secure Communication Platforms: Blockchain could be used to create communication platforms where all messages are encrypted and stored on a blockchain. This would provide a high level of security and privacy, and could be used for everything from business communications to social messaging apps.

Data Marketplace: A blockchain platform could allow individuals to securely sell or rent valuable data to companies. The data would be encrypted and the individual would control who has access to it. This could provide a more secure and privacy-respecting alternative to the current data broker models.

Decentralized Cloud Storage: Blockchain could be used to create a decentralized and secure cloud storage service. Users' files would be encrypted and split into pieces across the network, ensuring that no single party has control over the data.

Digital Rights Management: Artists and content creators could use blockchain to control and monetize their work. Each piece of content could be encrypted and stored on a blockchain, with a smart contract managing access and payment.

Supply Chain Security: Companies could use blockchain to securely track products as they move through a supply chain. Each step in the process could be recorded on the blockchain, with the data encrypted to protect business-sensitive information.

Efficiency

Despite being slower than other technologies for data storage, blockchains are much more efficient in other ways.

Transactions

Each *write* is a *transaction.* In other words, when you want to do something, you specify all the steps, and unless all steps succeed, the transaction is aborted and nothing gets written. This is very important in business and often requires special external services, like escrow.

Without the need for intermediaries, transactions and processes can be carried out faster and more smoothly. This drastically reduces the time required for reconciliation and dispute resolution.

When combined with the transparency of the blockchain, this process removes difficulties in tracking data. For example, in a supply chain context, a blockchain could provide real-time, trustworthy information about the location and status of goods, dramatically speeding up the process and reducing the risk of errors or fraud.

Smart Contracts

A huge part of efficiency is the ability to write and execute smart contracts, or coded rules of transactions. You can specify what happens when this code is called, who can call it and what it should do. Users can automate very complex processes and agreements, reducing the potential for errors and delays and without having to rely on third parties. We will discuss this in detail later.

Immutability

An important part of the design of any blockchain is the difficulty of manipulating stored data. Complicated algorithms are deployed in order to make such manipulation impossible. If you want to research further, look into Proof of Stake and Proof of Work, for example.

The guarantee that once a transaction is completed it is timestamped, with extreme precision, and is forever a part of the chain is extremely useful.

Blockchain immutability can offer strong benefits in terms of data integrity and transparency. However, it also poses challenges in terms of data privacy and rectification rights—particularly in jurisdictions subject to regulations like the EU's General Data Protection Regulation (GDPR). Any business model based on blockchain immutability needs to carefully consider these aspects.

This feature opens up a wealth of opportunities for various types of businesses. Here are a few examples:

Digital Notary Services: Companies can provide blockchain-based notary services where documents can be timestamped and stored in an immutable way. Any changes to the original document would be recorded as new transactions, making it easy to track edits and prove authenticity.

Intellectual Property Rights Management: The blockchain could be used to create a tamper-proof system for registering and tracking intellectual property rights, like patents, copyrights, or trademarks. This would give creators a concrete way to prove ownership and potentially combat infringement.

Academic Credential Verification: Educational institutions or third-party companies could issue degrees, diplomas, and other credentials on a blockchain. This would create an immutable record of a person's academic achievements, which could then be easily verified by employers or other interested parties.

Immutable Auditing and Compliance Platforms: In sectors with stringent auditing or regulatory compliance requirements (such as finance, healthcare, or manufacturing), blockchain could be used to record key data or transactions in an immutable way. This could simplify the auditing process and provide stronger assurances of compliance.

Decentralized Autonomous Organizations (DAOs): These are member-owned communities without a centralized authority. All decisions, rules, and financial transactions in a DAO are recorded on an immutable blockchain, which helps ensure transparency and fairness.

Immutable Identity Platforms: Blockchain could be used to create immutable digital identities. This could help reduce identity theft and fraud, and could be used in a variety of contexts, from online login systems to border control.

Supply Chain Management: By using a blockchain to record every step of a product's journey from manufacture to sale, companies can create an immutable and transparent record that can help reduce fraud, increase efficiency, and build consumer trust.

Decentralization

Databases can vary greatly in their distribution and failover capabilities. Let's create a categorization:

Single Server Databases: These databases run on a single server. They do not have inherent distribution or failover capabilities, but may be paired with additional software for backup and recovery. Example databases in this category include SQLite and Microsoft Access.
The main bottleneck here is the single server itself. If it goes down, the entire database becomes inaccessible. Additionally, as all reads and writes must go through this server, it can become a performance bottleneck if the workload exceeds the server's capacity.

Master-Slave Replication Databases: In this setup, one database server (the "master") is primarily responsible for handling writes, while one or more other servers (the "slaves") replicate the master's data and handle read queries. If the master fails, one of the slaves can take over, but manual intervention is typically required. MySQL and PostgreSQL are common examples of databases that can be set up in a master-slave configuration.

The master server is a potential point of failure and performance bottleneck, as it handles all write operations. If the master goes down, manual intervention is typically needed to promote a slave to master, during which time write operations cannot be processed.

Multi-Master Replication Databases: In this configuration, multiple database servers (masters) can handle write operations. This can provide higher availability and better performance, but it also introduces complexity due to the potential for conflicts if the same data is updated on different masters at the same time. MySQL with NDB Cluster and CouchDB are examples of databases that support multi-master replication.

Although this setup alleviates the master as a single point of failure, it introduces the complexity of conflict resolution when the same data is updated on different masters concurrently. Also, network latency and bandwidth can become a bottleneck when synchronizing data across multiple masters.

Distributed Databases (Sharding): These databases can distribute data across multiple servers or nodes. Each node handles a subset of the data, which can provide better performance and scalability. However, complex queries that involve multiple shards can be challenging. Examples include MongoDB (with sharding enabled), Google Cloud Spanner, and Amazon DynamoDB.

The potential bottlenecks in a sharded database depend on the distribution of data. If data is unevenly distributed, some shards might end up processing a disproportionate amount of queries, leading to performance issues. Additionally, queries that involve multiple shards can be slow due to the need to aggregate data across the network. A central authority for routing and coordination could potentially be a single point of failure.

Distributed Databases (Replication): These databases can replicate data across multiple nodes, each of which can handle reads and writes. This can provide high availability and fault tolerance. Examples include Cassandra and Riak.

While these databases provide high availability and fault tolerance, they can face bottlenecks in terms of network latency and bandwidth, particularly if the data needs to be replicated to a large number of nodes. Also, maintaining consistency across all nodes can be challenging and could potentially impact performance.

Distributed SQL Databases: These databases aim to combine the scalability and fault tolerance of NoSQL distributed databases with the strong consistency and structured query language (SQL) of traditional relational databases. Examples include Google Spanner, CockroachDB, and TiDB.

These databases face similar potential bottlenecks as other distributed databases, including network latency, bandwidth, and the complexity of maintaining consistency across nodes. However, they strive to mitigate these issues by offering strong consistency and SQL support, which can simplify application development. Some systems may rely on a central authority for coordination, which could be a point of failure.

Decentralized Databases: These databases extend the concept of distribution even further, with no central authority or single point of failure. Data is stored across numerous nodes, potentially spread across the globe. Blockchain can be considered a form of decentralized database.

These databases aim to eliminate any single point of failure by distributing data across a large number of nodes without a central authority. However, this can introduce complexity in terms of data consistency and conflict resolution. Additionally, network latency and bandwidth can become significant bottlenecks, especially given the potentially large number of nodes involved in confirming transactions in systems like blockchain.

Disclaimer: Keep in mind that the categorization and capabilities can vary based on the specific configuration and setup. For example, many databases can be configured for replication or sharding depending on the use case, and may support different levels of consistency, performance, and fault tolerance. Additionally, many modern databases support a hybrid model, offering features from multiple categories.

Blockchains can be configured to run a specific set or number of nodes or be open ended. As long as the nodes can follow the agreed-upon protocol and communicate with other nodes, this system has no size limit. Each node can have all or partial data and can run on any device, be written in any language and use any tech stack.

So what does the "every node for itself" structure of blockchain buy us? The ability to synchronize across the world. If nodes can see any other nodes, they can synchronize. Once the nodes have data, queries can be run on it, and that data can be used and retrieved. Any and all nodes can be up constantly or intermittently. Once up, they will catch up to the latest blocks available.

This makes a blockchain impossible to regulate and lock out. Some of these technologies have deep roots in Napster, Tor and other questionable businesses that were designed to escape oversight and boundaries. Who knew they were creating the future of distributed networks that are making such a huge impact so many years later?

Examples:

Decentralized Finance (DeFi) Platforms: These platforms use blockchain technology to recreate traditional financial systems like lending, borrowing, and trading in a decentralized manner, eliminating the need for intermediaries. Examples include Uniswap for decentralized exchange, Compound for lending and borrowing, and MakerDAO for stablecoin and decentralized governance.

Decentralized Marketplaces: These marketplaces leverage the power of blockchain to directly connect buyers and sellers without an intermediary. OpenBazaar is an example of a decentralized marketplace where you can trade goods and services freely.

Decentralized Data Storage Networks: Traditional cloud storage services are centralized and owned by a single entity. Blockchain can enable the creation of decentralized data storage networks, like Filecoin or Storj, where anyone can rent out their unused storage space.

Decentralized Identity Platforms: Blockchain can be used to create a system for self-sovereign identity, where individuals maintain control over their personal data. Companies like Civic provide secure identity verification services on the blockchain.

Decentralized Content Distribution Networks: Blockchain can be used to create a decentralized platform for sharing and monetizing content. LBRY, for example, is a blockchain-based platform for sharing digital content, with its own cryptocurrency for rewarding creators.

IoT devices have suffered for years from being easily hacked, due to stripped-down software and hardware. One of the biggest angles of attack has been their failure to verify authentic firmware, allowing EvilCorps to upload their own and enlist an innocent $10 power outlet in your house to seed ransomware or spy on network activity. If manufacturers switched to a decentralized content distribution network, this would no longer be a threat vector (unless poorly implemented).

Decentralized Internet Infrastructure: Blockchain can also be used to create decentralized versions of key internet infrastructure. For example, Handshake is a decentralized, permissionless naming protocol compatible with the Domain Name System (DNS), and Orchid offers a decentralized virtual private network (VPN). There have been many recent DNS attacks, so blockchain is a natural progression.

Trustless Transactions

Blockchain were designed to allow parties that do not trust each other to transact in a secure and verifiable way without intermediaries. This can be particularly beneficial in peer-to-peer marketplaces, finance, supply chain relationships, or any other transaction where trust is a concern.

We don't mean "move crypto to a broker-dealer that pretends they have an exchange, then transact." We are talking about the native ability of the platform to do so.

Smart contracts take this a step further, allowing users to implement rules and workflows around transactions, usually in an effort to make them trustless.

While blockchains can eliminate the need for trust in many cases, it also presents its own challenges and risks, such as smart contract bugs or exploits, volatile cryptocurrency prices, and regulatory uncertainty. Any business model based on trustless transactions needs to consider these factors.

Decentralized Exchanges (DEX): Platforms like Uniswap or SushiSwap allow users to trade digital assets directly from their wallets, without needing to trust an intermediary to hold their assets or execute their trades. The rules of the exchange are encoded in smart contracts, creating a trustless trading environment.

Smart Contracts for Escrow Services: In traditional transactions, an escrow agent is often used to hold assets or funds on behalf of the parties involved, releasing them only once certain conditions are met. With blockchain and smart contracts, the escrow process can be automated and made trustless. The smart contract only releases the funds when the agreed-upon conditions are met, eliminating the need for a trusted third party.

Supply Chain Traceability: Blockchain can be used to create a transparent and tamper-proof record of a product's journey from production to sale. Each participant in the supply chain—manufacturers, distributors, retailers—adds their information to the product's record on the blockchain. This creates a trustless system for verifying the authenticity and origin of products, helping to combat counterfeiting and fraud.

Decentralized Finance (DeFi): DeFi protocols like Compound or Aave create trustless environments for lending and borrowing. Rather than trusting a bank or other financial institution to manage loans and deposits, users interact directly with smart contracts on the blockchain. The terms of each loan, including interest rates and collateral requirements, are enforced automatically by the smart contracts.

Decentralized Autonomous Organizations (DAOs): In a DAO, decisions are made by the community according to preset rules encoded in smart contracts. This creates a trustless system for governance, as decisions are made transparently and automatically, without the need for a trusted central authority.

Prediction Markets: Blockchain-based prediction markets, like Augur, allow users to bet on the outcome of events in a trustless manner. Payouts are determined and distributed automatically by smart contracts, without the need for a trusted intermediary.

Gambling: You create a contract that says, for example, if a random number is even, the first party wins and if odd, the second party wins. Now anyone can use that contract and they don't need to trust the other party or the dealer to pay and not cheat. It's safer than real-life gambling.

Decentralized Trading: Trustless transactions on the blockchain would ensure that all trades are fair and transparent, and smart contracts could handle the automated buying/selling based on demand and supply.

Decentralized Health Record Management: A platform could use blockchain to securely and privately store individuals' health records. Trustless transactions would ensure that only authorized individuals could access or add to a patient's records, with each transaction transparently logged for accountability.

Decentralized Job Marketplaces: A job marketplace could use blockchain to create a trustless environment for freelancers and employers. Smart contracts could handle the agreement between parties, and automatically release payment once job completion is verified. This could remove the need for a central platform that takes a percentage of the freelancer's earnings.

Decentralized Insurance: Blockchain could be used to create a peer-to-peer insurance platform, where individuals pool their resources to cover claims. Smart contracts would automatically handle claim payouts based on pre-agreed conditions, removing the need for an insurance company as an intermediary.

Decentralized Real Estate Transactions: The entire process of buying or selling real estate could be handled on a blockchain platform. Trustless transactions would ensure fair and transparent dealing, and smart contracts could automatically handle the transfer of property rights once payment is received.

Decentralized Art Verification and Ownership: Blockchain could be used to create a platform for verifying the authenticity and ownership of artworks. Each piece of art could be linked to a unique token on the blockchain, and the transfer of this token in a trustless transaction would represent the transfer of ownership of the artwork.

Automation and Smart Contracts

Smart contracts are self-executing programmed contracts where the terms of the agreement are directly written into lines of code. These allow for a high degree of automation in processes, which can reduce the need for manual oversight and speed up transaction times.

The process is straightforward:

- The blockchain defines rules about how smart contracts are coded, deployed and executed.
- You follow the standard software development process.
- The code is reviewed and tested.
- The code is deployed to the blockchain.
- Parts of the code can be automatically executed based on another's actions or executed directly by the end user.

The possibilities of smart contracts are vast and continue to expand as blockchain technology matures and more use cases are explored. Entire workflows can be defined in a smart contract. If you can code it—and it's mathematically proven that anything can be coded—you can do it. Here are just some of the things you can do with a smart contract:

Transfer of Value: A smart contract can be programmed to transfer digital assets, such as cryptocurrencies or tokens, between parties, often upon the fulfillment of certain conditions. For instance, in a betting scenario, the contract could automatically transfer the bet amount to the winning party once the outcome is known.

Manage Permissions: A smart contract can be used to manage permissions within a blockchain network. For instance, it could specify who has the rights to perform certain actions, like adding data to the blockchain or voting in a decision-making process.

Execute Business Logic: Just as a traditional contract defines rules and penalties surrounding an agreement, a smart contract can encode business logic that executes automatically when certain conditions are met. For example, a supply-chain smart contract could automatically register a product as delivered once its GPS location matches the delivery address.

Automate Financial Services: In decentralized finance (DeFi), smart contracts replicate traditional financial services—such as lending, borrowing, and earning interest—in a fully automated and decentralized manner. For example, a smart contract on a lending platform might automatically adjust interest rates based on supply and demand.

Create Digital Assets: Smart contracts can be used to create digital assets or tokens. These tokens can represent a wide range of tangible and intangible assets, such as real estate, company shares, or access rights to a service.

Decentralized Autonomous Organizations (DAOs): A smart contract can encode the rules for a DAO, a type of organization that is run by rules encoded in smart contracts. It could determine voting rights, profit sharing, and other governance mechanisms.

Escrow Services: Smart contracts can function as trustless escrow systems. For instance, in a marketplace, a smart contract could temporarily hold funds from a buyer until the seller has delivered the goods or services.

Conditional Payments: Smart contracts can facilitate conditional payments based on external data. For example, a crop insurance smart contract could automatically compensate farmers if a certain weather condition, such as a drought, is recorded by a trusted data source.

Decentralized Gaming: Smart contracts can facilitate trustless, decentralized gaming experiences. In a blockchain-based chess game, for instance, the smart contract could automatically enforce the rules of the game, record each move on the blockchain, and transfer a predefined amount of cryptocurrency from the loser to the winner.

Virtual Reality Worlds: Blockchain-based virtual reality platforms, such as Decentraland, use smart contracts to manage property ownership within the virtual world. Users can purchase parcels of virtual land, represented by tokens, and the transfer of these tokens is handled by a smart contract.

Fantasy Sports: Smart contracts can be used to automate the operations of fantasy sports leagues. The contract could handle the distribution of winnings, manage trades between players, and enforce the league's rules without needing a centralized authority.

Art Creation and Auctions: With smart contracts, artists can create digital art (represented by NFTs) that can be bought, sold, and auctioned. The smart contract could automatically transfer ownership of the NFT to the highest bidder, and even provide the artist with a percentage of the proceeds every time their work is resold.

Decentralized Music Platforms: Smart contracts can be used to create a music platform where artists upload their music directly, and listeners pay them directly. The smart contract could automatically split payments between all contributors to a song (like producers, writers, and musicians) according to predefined percentages.

Decentralized Betting: Smart contracts can facilitate decentralized, peer-to-peer betting platforms. For instance, a group of friends could bet on the outcome of a sports game. The smart contract would hold all the stakes, and once the game is over, it would automatically distribute the winnings to the right people based on the game's outcome.

Decentralized Film and Video Platforms: Similar to the music platform, a video platform could use smart contracts to handle the automatic splitting of payments to all contributors of a film or video. This could also be applied to streaming services, where users pay for the content they watch, and the payment is automatically split between all parties involved.

Collectible Games: Games like CryptoKitties use smart contracts to create unique, collectible digital pets. Each CryptoKitty is an NFT, representing a unique digital cat with its own set of characteristics. The game's smart contract handles breeding, buying, and selling of these digital pets.

Cost Reduction

This goes hand-in-hand with efficiency, but its impact is much more straightforward.

Overhead Costs: Running a corporate database server usually requires a database administrator and a data center. Operating and maintaining the database demands considerable labor for tasks like creating backups, performing restores and monitoring uptime. A blockchain merely requires a managed service that typically charges only for data deposits.

Transaction Costs: It currently costs $20 to $40 to wire money globally from one bank to another. Transactions in bitcoin, ether, and stablecoins cost a tiny fraction of that, even before considering that multiple transactions can be compressed into one for significant cost savings.

This is due to:

Reduction of Intermediaries: Traditional business networks often involve multiple intermediaries—banks, lawyers, brokers, etc.—to establish trust and perform essential functions. Blockchain, with its inherent trust and transparency, can eliminate the need for these intermediaries, thereby reducing costs and transaction times.

Automation via Smart Contracts: Smart contracts on a blockchain can automate business processes, thereby reducing the need for manual intervention and associated labor costs. For example, supply chain processes can be automated from manufacturing to delivery, with payments released automatically upon the fulfillment of predefined conditions.

Improved Audit and Compliance: Blockchain provides an immutable, transparent record of all transactions. This simplifies auditing and reduces costs associated with regulatory compliance.

Streamlined Payments: Blockchain can simplify and reduce the cost of transferring funds, especially in cross-border transactions, which often involve currency exchange fees and delays. Cryptocurrencies can be transferred globally swiftly and at a fraction of the cost of traditional wire transfers.

Reduced Fraud: Due to its decentralized and tamper-proof nature, blockchain can significantly reduce fraud, particularly in sectors like finance or supply chains where fraudulent activities can be costly.

Efficient Supply Chain Management: By providing a single, transparent version of product history, blockchain can reduce the time and cost involved in tracking and verifying goods as they move through the supply chain, thus minimizing disputes and delays.

Costs of Data Management: Centralized databases can be expensive to maintain and secure. A blockchain-based data management system is not only more secure but also less costly, as data storage is shared across all participants in the network.

Business Ideas

Some ideas for businesses that could revolutionize the established monopolies:

Independent Music Labels or Movie Studios: By employing blockchain technology, these entities could streamline the distribution of royalties, ensuring artists are paid both fairly and promptly whenever their music or movies are played.

Local Agriculture Co-ops: These could utilize blockchain for traceability of produce from farm to table, enhancing transparency and accountability while appealing to consumers who value knowing the source of their food.

Independent News Organizations: Blockchain could facilitate a more transparent system for tracking news sources, thereby reducing misinformation and increasing trust.

Small to Medium Enterprises (SMEs) in Manufacturing: These could benefit from more efficient supply chain management, reducing both the time and cost associated with tracking and verifying the movement of goods.

Professional Service Providers: Lawyers, consultants, and other professionals could use smart contracts to automate agreement enforcement and streamline payments, making their services more efficient and potentially more appealing to clients.

Local Energy Producers: Small-scale renewable energy producers could use blockchain to facilitate peer-to-peer energy trading, thereby improving efficiency and reducing costs.

Independent Educational Institutions: These could use blockchain to issue tamper-proof degrees and certificates, enhancing their credibility and reducing potential for fraud.

Specialty Insurance Providers: Such firms could use smart contracts to automate claims processing, making their services more efficient and customer-friendly.

Innovation in Public Services: Governments and public sector organizations could use blockchain for tasks ranging from managing land registries to administering social welfare programs, thereby reducing fraud and increasing efficiency.

Decentralized Clinical Trials: Healthcare and pharmaceutical companies could employ blockchain to conduct clinical trials with enhanced data security and integrity. This could also aid in patient recruitment and consent management and may reduce the size and scope of future lawsuits.

Interoperability and Standardization

Blockchains themselves are great examples of interoperability and standardization. First, a specification is written, describing how nodes communicate, how to decode the data, which encryption methods are used, and other parameters. Then, anyone is free to implement a node or create tools around it using any tech stack they desire.

Pick any language—C#, C++, Java, Go, Python, Ruby, Rust, Kotlin, Scala, or any other you'd like. Developing according to a well-documented protocol allows for higher security, greater oversight, and a polished final product.

What emerges is a standard system for communication and data storage, along with a standardized way to codify workflows via smart contracts. With blockchain, we have a multitude of prebuilt pieces that are already written, tested, and functional:

:

Messaging Bus/System	Cryptography
Peer-to-Peer Network	Smart Contracts
Consensus Mechanism	Distributed Ledger

Transaction Processor

Wallets

Interoperability Protocols

Identity Management

Security Protocols

Governance Mechanisms

Data Validation

Error Handling and Recovery

Transaction Pool

API Interfaces

Blockchain Explorers

Oracle Services

Tokenization Systems

Privacy Layers

Cross-Chain Bridges

Layer 2 Solutions

Version Control

Scaling Solutions

Monitoring and Analytics Tools

Backup and Redundancy Systems

Node Operation and Management

Hash Functions

Asset Management

Timestamping Services

Decentralized File and Data Storage

Not only can we use and reuse any of these features for building other projects, but we also have the flexibility of using the blockchain as a whole.

Define a standard for how you will store data and publish it to your industry and users. Once you have a properly documented, publicly available API, design it for others to use. Now you've established an industry standard, paving the way for greater achievements.

Standardization positions blockchains to serve as a shared, universal infrastructure, enabling greater interoperability among systems and organizations. This is particularly useful in fragmented industries like healthcare, where data interoperability poses a significant challenge. Such standardization can benefit companies and entire industries, especially in data exchange and storage.

When different systems can communicate seamlessly, it simplifies information exchange, reducing both time and cost associated with data reconciliation. With blockchain, data is recorded in a standard format across all network nodes, ensuring everyone is working with identical data. This is especially beneficial in industries where multiple parties need to interact with that data.

For instance, in a supply chain involving multiple parties (manufacturers, shippers, retailers, etc.), using a standard blockchain protocol ensures all parties view the same data, thereby reducing the potential for disputes and the need for manual reconciliation. This can result in significant cost savings, as resolving disputes and reconciling data can be both time-consuming and expensive.

Furthermore, blockchain standardization can mitigate the risk of poor data design and management. Traditional databases often store data in varied formats across different organizations or systems, leading to inconsistencies and potential errors. In contrast, a standardized blockchain protocol ensures data is recorded and stored in a consistent, tamper-proof manner. This can decrease the risk of data errors and improve overall data quality, which is vital for decision-making processes.

Moreover, blockchain technology offers enhanced data security. Because of its decentralized nature, data is not stored in a single location but is distributed across a network of computers, reducing the risk of data loss or hacking. Coupled with cryptographic techniques, this can substantially improve data security, adding an extra layer of protection to sensitive information. Ransomware cannot delete your pictures and documents if they are on a blockchain; each node serves as both a backup and a restoration mechanism, allowing other nodes to upgrade and rewrite themselves as necessary.

Lastly, adopting blockchain standardization can simplify regulatory compliance for industries. A clear, standard format for data recording and storage allows industries to comply more easily with data management and privacy regulations, thereby reducing the risk of noncompliance and associated penalties. Data can be stored encrypted, if necessary—simply hand the decryption keys and tools to the auditors.

The interoperability and standardization features of blockchain technology offer more efficient, secure, and cost-effective data exchange and storage, presenting significant advantages for companies and industries. However, implementing these features requires careful consideration of the associated technical, regulatory, and organizational challenges.

Some business ideas that capitalize on data standardization:

IoT Data Management Companies: In the Internet of Things (IoT) ecosystem, countless devices generate a massive amount of data that needs to be securely and efficiently managed. An IoT data management company could leverage blockchain technology to standardize and securely store data from disparate IoT devices.

For instance, in a smart city scenario, data from traffic lights, public transport systems, waste management facilities, energy grids, and more could be integrated into a standardized format using blockchain. This would enhance the interoperability of these systems, allowing for more coordinated and efficient operations, predictive maintenance, and improved public services. The decentralized nature of blockchain also adds an extra layer of security, making the data resistant to single points of failure.

Precision Agriculture: Businesses in this sector could use blockchain for cross-company data sharing about soil quality, weather patterns, and crop performance. This could lead to improved crop-yield predictions and more efficient resource use.

Healthcare Data Aggregators: Such companies could use blockchain to gather data from healthcare providers, enabling better research while preserving patient privacy. Achieving this would require interoperability with various healthcare data systems.

Real Estate MLS Services: Multiple Listing Services could greatly benefit from blockchain standardization, making property data sharing more reliable and transparent across real estate agencies and enhancing the quality of service for buyers and sellers.

Cross-Border NGOs: Nongovernmental organizations working across borders could use blockchain to standardize the data they collect, making it easier to analyze and report on their activities.

Supply Chain Auditing Firms: These firms could use blockchain to ensure that data from multiple sources is consistent and reliable. This is particularly important in industries such as fashion and electronics, where verifying ethical sourcing can be challenging.

Decentralized AI Training Platforms: These platforms could use blockchain to collect and standardize data from numerous sources, ensuring that the trained models are robust and diversified.

Cultural Heritage Organizations: Blockchain could be used to create a standardized and tamper-proof registry of cultural artifacts, aiding in their preservation and tracking.

Environmental Data Services: Companies specializing in collecting and analyzing environmental data could use blockchain to standardize data from different sources, making it easier to track environmental changes and predict future trends.

Digital Credentialing Services: These companies could use blockchain to standardize and verify digital credentials, simplifying the process for individuals to prove their skills and for employers to verify these credentials.

Autonomous Vehicle Networks: Companies operating in this domain could use blockchain to standardize the data exchanged between autonomous vehicles, enhancing their ability to navigate and interact safely.

Tokenization and Digital Assets

Now we come to the most popular and potentially scandalous feature of a blockchain: tracking the ownership of assets.

This "anyone can do it" technology has enabled many successes and also many scams. It's a fantastic piece of tech.

So ... How Does It Work?

From an IT architect's perspective, tokenization is the process of converting rights to an asset into a digital token on a blockchain. This process creates an environment in which transactions are secure, quick, and independent of a central authority.

Tokenization allows for the creation of unique identifiers for assets, significantly enhancing traceability and security. This is particularly useful in scenarios such as supply chain management, where items can be traced from production to the end consumer, and in data security, where sensitive information is tokenized to mitigate the risk of breaches.

Implementation varies from one blockchain to another, but at the core is a table of addresses. Each location in the table typically stores a numerical value representing a percentage or number of shares, tokens, or other assets.

Often, coded contracts will enforce rules addressing questions like: Can we print more of these tokens? Can we freeze individual accounts or even all transactions for this token (useful during a presale)? When should users be allowed to transfer funds on their own (also useful during a presale)? And so on.

For businesses, the benefits are manifold. Tokenization enables them to convert virtually any asset—be it physical or intangible—into a digital token with verifiable ownership that can be easily and securely traded and tracked. This can include anything from a piece of real estate and shares in a company to intellectual property or even a person's time, opening up new markets and democratizing access to investment opportunities traditionally available only to a select few.

Digital assets, such as cryptocurrencies or NFTs, provide new ways of handling value and ownership. They can serve as a medium of exchange, a unit of account, and a store of value—all without the need for intermediaries. This can significantly reduce costs and expedite transactions, enabling new business models. For example, artists can sell their work directly to consumers as NFTs, retaining more of the value they create.

Moreover, tokenization can facilitate fractional ownership, making assets more affordable and liquid. For instance, tokenizing a piece of real estate could allow multiple investors to own and trade shares in the property, broadening access to the real estate market (laws of jurisdiction permitting).

Tokenization and digital assets introduce a new level of flexibility, security, and inclusivity in managing and trading assets, enabling IT architects and businesses to explore innovative approaches to value and ownership.

Advanced Use Cases

Say you have formed a firm that needs to track partial ownership in an asset. You bought a building or a work of art and you expect a bunch of people to want to own parts of it and trade them. What do you need to do to make this real?

Designing a Web3 product for trading tokenized assets involves at least these steps:

1. **Define the Asset**: Identify and define the asset you wish to tokenize. This could be a physical object, a digital asset, intellectual property, a service, or virtually any other form of value.

2. **Get in Compliance**: Understand and comply with relevant regulations in your jurisdiction. Consult with legal counsel to ensure your tokenized asset does not constitute a security unless you are prepared to meet the associated regulatory requirements.

3. **Select a Blockchain**: Choose the blockchain that will host your tokenized asset. Consider factors such as transaction speed, cost, community support, level of decentralization, and compatibility with the standards used for your token.

4. **Design Your Token**: Decide whether the token will be fungible (identical to others, like a cryptocurrency) or non-fungible (unique, like an NFT). Define the properties of the token and its relationship to the underlying asset.

5. **Develop Smart Contracts**: Develop the smart contracts governing your token's behavior. This may include functions for "minting" and "burning" tokens, transferring tokens between wallets, and potentially integrating with external systems.

6. **Conduct a Security Audit**: Have your smart contracts audited by a third party to ensure they are free of vulnerabilities that could be exploited. This is crucial, as contracts are difficult to update and data is hard to roll back in the event of a bug.

7. **Mint Your Tokens**: Create your tokens on the blockchain and prepare them for distribution.

8. **Build a Web3 Interface**: Develop a Web3-enabled website or app where users can interact with your tokenized assets. This may include displaying token properties, facilitating the buying and selling of tokens, and integrating with wallet software for self-management by users.

9. **Consider Identity and Access Management**: Determine how users will authenticate and what types of access controls will be required. Consider integrating with wallet-based identity solutions for a seamless Web3 experience.

10. **Provide Liquidity**: If you're creating a market for your token, consider how you'll initially provide liquidity. You may need to collaborate with a liquidity provider or establish a liquidity pool yourself.

11. **Build a Community**: Develop a strategy to market your tokenized asset and build a community around it. Tactics might include social media promotion, partnerships, influencer marketing, and direct outreach to potential users.

12. **Plan Your Customer Support Strategy**: Users may have questions or encounter issues, and timely, effective support can be crucial to your product's success.

13. **Keep It Running**: After launch, monitor your product's performance and user feedback, and plan for updates, improvements, and potential scaling issues.

This is a complex process that requires a blend of technical, legal, and business expertise. It's important to take the time to plan thoroughly and ensure that you're building a product that's secure, compliant, and valuable to your users.

Zero-Knowledge Proof Mechanisms

Good blockchains allow you to code your own rules. You are limited only by your imagination. Say you don't want to store some values openly in the blockchain for everyone to see? You can simply store references or mappings to another system, or encrypt your data. Obfuscation is easy when you're the one coding the rules.

One of the most exciting developments in cryptography lately has been the advent of zero-knowledge proof.

Zero-knowledge proofs (ZKPs) are cryptographic methods by which one party (the prover) can prove to another party (the verifier) that they know a value or a secret without conveying any information apart from the fact that they indeed know the secret.

In the context of the tokenization of digital assets, ZKPs can provide a robust layer of privacy and security. For example, a user could prove that they have enough tokens to make a purchase without revealing exactly how many tokens they have. This can maintain user privacy and create a more secure environment for digital transactions.

Suppose you have two piles of marbles, both too big to count by eye, and you are the only one who knows how many you started with. You want to prove to a friend that these two piles have the same number of marbles, but you don't want to reveal how many marbles are in the piles.

You ask your friend to turn around so they can't see what you're doing. While your friend isn't looking, you add an equal number of marbles to both piles. You then tell your friend they can look again and remove an equal number of marbles, as many as they like, from each pile.

No matter how many marbles your friend removes, both piles always have the same number of marbles left. By doing this, your friend can confirm that both piles started with the same number of marbles, even though they never found out the actual number of marbles in each pile.

In the context of digital assets, this method could be used to prove that two accounts have the same amount of a specific token without revealing the actual amount held in each account.

Types of Tokens and Coins

There are several types of tokens in the blockchain space, each serving a distinct function. Here are a few types:

Security Tokens: Like a share of stock, these tokens derive their value from an external, tradable asset. They often represent shares in a company, profits, or voting rights. Security tokens are subject to federal securities laws, including the requirement to register offerings with the Securities and Exchange Commission.

The legal test determining whether a token is a security is called the Howey Test, named after the 1946 Supreme Court case *SEC v. W. J. Howey Co.* Under the Howey Test, a transaction is considered a securities transaction if it involves an investment of money in a common enterprise, with the expectation of profit derived from the efforts of others.

Utility Tokens: These tokens provide users with access to a product or service. They are often used within a specific blockchain ecosystem. For example, ether is a utility token used to pay for transaction fees and computational services on the Ethereum network.

If you plan to issue a utility token to raise money for your project while avoiding securities regulation, exercise extreme caution. A common mistake with utility tokens is promising a stable value while offering discounts, which may risk the token being categorized as a security. Consult your legal team if you're considering this route.

Stablecoins: These tokens are designed to minimize volatility by pegging their value to a reserve of assets, such as a specific amount of a fiat currency like the U.S. dollar, a different cryptocurrency, or even a commodity like gold.

Governance Tokens: These tokens allow holders to vote on decisions that affect the protocol or platform. They provide a means for decentralized autonomous organizations (DAOs) to make collective decisions.

Non-Fungible Tokens (NFTs): These are unique tokens that represent ownership of a unique item or piece of content. They cannot be directly replaced by any other token; they are *non-fungible*.

NFTs also have other uses, such as representing membership or granting access to an online resource or real-world venue.

Asset Tokens: These tokens represent ownership of an underlying asset, like real estate or commodities. They form part of tokenization, where physical assets are digitally represented.

Payment Tokens: These are cryptocurrencies primarily used for transactions, like bitcoin. Their main purpose is to serve as a medium of exchange.

The category into which a token falls can affect its legal standing, its potential uses, and its tax treatment. Always consult with a knowledgeable professional if you're unsure.

This list will never be complete, as people will continually conceive new ways to use available mechanisms to emulate, imitate, or enhance life.

So What Can You Do With All This Information?

You can tokenize anything:

Tokenized Loyalty Programs: Airlines, supermarkets, and other businesses could tokenize their loyalty points, such as airline miles. This would enable customers to trade these tokens, potentially even across different platforms, adding a new level of flexibility to loyalty programs. Customers could truly own their loyalty points and decide how and where they want to use or trade them.

Art Tokenization Platforms: Platforms enabling artists to tokenize their artworks, providing a new way to sell and track their creations.

Decentralized Real Estate Platforms: These platforms could allow fractional ownership of properties through tokenization, expanding access to the real estate market.

Tokenized Intellectual Property Rights Management: Businesses can manage and monetize intellectual property rights, such as music, writing, or patents, by tokenizing them.

Decentralized E-Commerce Platforms: E-commerce platforms where products are tokenized, creating a unique identity and history for each product.

Decentralized Financing: Independent filmmakers could tokenize and sell shares in their films to raise funds and allow investors to earn returns from the film's profits.

Decentralized Research Platforms: Academics and researchers could tokenize their research findings, allowing them to profit from their work and control how it's used.

You can make anything into a market:

Decentralized Gaming Platforms: Gaming companies could tokenize in-game assets, enabling players to own, trade, or sell these assets outside of the game itself. This could revolutionize the gaming industry by providing gamers with tangible value from their in-game achievements, and possibly even allowing the exchange of assets between games on the same platform.

Digital Collectibles Marketplaces: Marketplaces where users can create, sell, and trade tokenized collectibles.

Tokenized Personal Services: Platforms where individuals can tokenize and sell their personal services, like consultancy hours, personal training sessions, or cooking classes.

Crowdfunding Platforms for Startups: These platforms could use tokenization to provide backers with fractional ownership of the projects they support.

Decentralized Trading Platforms: companies could enable customers to tokenize and trade anything, from excess energy they've generated from solar panels to tokenized assets to debt.

Decentralized Lending Platforms: Platforms where borrowers and lenders can engage in peer-to-peer lending using tokenized assets as collateral.

Decentralized Personal Data Marketplaces: Platforms where individuals can tokenize and sell their personal data, maintaining control over who has access to their information.

Reality, via Oracles

In the context of blockchain technology, an oracle is a critical feature that enables a smart contract to interact with data and systems outside the blockchain. Simply put, an oracle acts as a messenger, providing real-world data to smart contracts on the blockchain.

By design, blockchains are closed systems that cannot access or verify external data on their own. They require a reliable method to interact with external information, particularly if this data is crucial for executing a smart contract.

Oracles serve this role, acting as a bridge between the blockchain and the real world. They supply the necessary external data to trigger smart contracts when predetermined conditions are met. For example, an oracle could provide temperature data from a weather station to a smart contract programmed to execute a transaction when the temperature reaches a specific level.

Various types of oracles exist, including software oracles, which import online data onto the blockchain; hardware oracles, which translate real-world events, such as sensor data, into a format the blockchain can interpret; and human oracles, who manually provide information to the blockchain.

It's important to note that while oracles are essential to blockchain technology, they introduce a level of trust into the system. The blockchain must trust that the oracle is supplying accurate and reliable data. This addition complicates the system and may pose security risks if not managed appropriately.

In some literature, oracles may also be called data feeds, data providers, or external data sources in the context of blockchain technology.

Here are the current players in this field. Given the relatively low entry cost, the landscape is likely to evolve over time.

Chainlink: Chainlink is the most widely recognized decentralized oracle network, allowing smart contracts on Ethereum to securely connect to external data sources, APIs, and payment systems. Chainlink is renowned for providing reliable, tamper-proof inputs and outputs for complex smart contracts across various blockchains.

Augur: Augur is a decentralized oracle and prediction market protocol built on the Ethereum blockchain. The platform enables users to forecast events and rewards accurate predictions.

Band Protocol: Operating on Cosmos but also compatible with Ethereum, Band Protocol links smart contracts to off-chain data and ensures data accuracy through a decentralized governance system.

Provable (formerly Oraclize): Provable offers data transport services, linking blockchain-based applications to web-based data. The service is blockchain-agnostic, supporting Ethereum, Bitcoin, and other chains.

Tellor: Tellor is an Ethereum-based decentralized oracle that features an on-chain data bank. Queries are staked in exchange for rewards.

Witnet: Witnet operates as a decentralized oracle network, connecting smart contracts to any online data source. The protocol uses a network of computers—known as "nodes" or "witnesses"—to retrieve data and rewards them for accurate provision.

Notably, Chainlink offers a widely used oracle service that includes a Verifiable Random Function (VRF). This function supplies smart contracts with a reliable source of randomness, using cryptographic proof to ensure each random number is genuine and untampered. This feature is especially useful in decentralized applications like gaming, where unbiased random numbers are essential for fair play.

The quest for "good" random numbers is crucial in computing applications and has long been a goal in software development. Given that blockchain users often rely on third parties for calculations and that trusting miners is generally not favored, implementing reliable randomness on a blockchain is challenging.

Here are some ideas for using oracle services.

Decentralized Insurance: A company could use oracle services to validate claims based on external data, such as weather data for crop insurance, flight data for travel insurance, or even data from human oracles such as trusted car mechanics.

Real Estate Platforms: A platform could use oracle data for property valuations, rental prices, or sale completions, enabling transparent and efficient property transactions.

Supply Chain Auditing Services: A service could validate data from multiple points in a supply chain, providing trustworthy audits and strengthening the supply chain's integrity.

Decentralized Energy Marketplaces: Such a marketplace could use oracle data for tracking energy production and consumption, enabling individuals to trade excess energy with their peers.

Sports Betting Platforms: A decentralized platform could use oracles to confirm sports outcomes and settle bets accordingly.

Predictive Analytics Firms: A firm could use oracle data in predictive models, selling forecasts for things like stock prices, climate patterns, or industry trends.

Crowdfunding Platforms: A platform could use oracles to validate whether project milestones have been met, ensuring funds are released on schedule.

Environmental Impact Tracking Services: A service could use oracles to provide verified data on companies' environmental impact, supporting more sustainable business practices.

Decentralized Freelance Platforms: Such a platform could use oracle services to verify project completion or hours worked, ensuring fair payment.

Customized News Platforms: A decentralized platform could curate news based on user preferences and feedback, using data from various online sources.

Innovation and Competitive Advantage

Implementing blockchain can be a source of competitive advantage, positioning an organization as an innovative leader in its field. It can also provide opportunities to develop new services or products based on the technology.

Every firm with a research and development department should take a hard look at the pros and cons of blockchains and how they could be used in their organization. Maybe this book will help some of them.

Every major technology utilized today has been a newcomer at some point, and for most it has been quite recently.

Social Media (Twitter) - Invented: 2006 - Widely Accepted: 2010s

Mobile Payment (Venmo) - Invented: 2009 - Widely Accepted: mid-2010s

Video Conferencing (Zoom) - Invented: 2011 - Widely Accepted: late 2010s

Blockchain (Bitcoin) - Invented: 2009 - Widely Accepted: late 2010s

Messaging Apps (WhatsApp) - Invented: 2009 - Widely Accepted: early 2010s

Ride Sharing (Lyft) - Invented: 2012 - Widely Accepted: mid-2010s

Streaming Music (Spotify) - Invented: 2008 - Widely Accepted: 2010s

Photo Sharing (Instagram) - Invented: 2010 - Widely Accepted: early 2010s

Augmented Reality (Pokemon Go) - Invented: 2016 - Widely Accepted: late 2010s

Online Workplaces (Slack) - Invented: 2013 - Widely Accepted: mid-2010s

Cloud-based Office Suite (Google Workspace) - Invented: 2006 - Widely Accepted: 2010s

Virtual Assistants (Amazon Alexa) - Invented: 2014 - Widely Accepted: late 2010s.

To be more specific to databases:

MySQL - Introduced: 1995 - Widely Accepted: early 2000s

PostgreSQL - Introduced: 1996 - Widely Accepted: mid-2000s

Microsoft SQL Server - Introduced: 1989 - Widely Accepted: mid-1990s

Oracle Database - Introduced: 1979 - Widely Accepted: mid-1980s

MongoDB - Introduced: 2009 - Widely Accepted: mid-2010s

SQLite - Introduced: 2000 - Widely Accepted: mid-2000s

Cassandra - Introduced: 2008 - Widely Accepted: early 2010s

Redis - Introduced: 2009 - Widely Accepted: early 2010s

Elasticsearch - Introduced: 2010 - Widely Accepted: mid-2010s

Firebase - Introduced: 2011 - Widely Accepted: mid-2010s

DynamoDB - Introduced: 2012 - Widely Accepted: mid-2010s

Neo4j - Introduced: 2007 - Widely Accepted: early 2010s.

Couchbase - Introduced: 2010 - Widely Accepted: early 2010s

Aurora (AWS) - Introduced: 2014 - Widely Accepted: late 2010s

Cosmos DB (Azure) - Introduced: 2017 - Widely Accepted: early 2020s.

It's easy to see that all of these are fairly recent. Many were incremental technology. It's easy to go from one SQL into another. Blockchain, on the other hand, is a total shift from traditional databases. And the agiotage around the coins likely hurt the technology more than it helped.

Chapter 3: All About Layers

In order to understand technology, it's often helpful to understand its layers. In an attempt to keep things high level, we'll pay the most attention here to their existence and less to how exactly they work.

Layers of Blockchains

In the blockchain space, we often discuss layers to describe different aspects of the technology and its operations. Here are the generally referenced layers:

Protocol Layer (Layer 1)

Also known as the base layer, the protocol layer serves as the foundation of blockchain technology. This layer governs block creation, transaction validation, consensus mechanisms, and network security. Examples of Layer 1 solutions include Bitcoin, Ethereum, and other standalone blockchains.

Network Layer

Responsible for transmitting messages—data and transactions—across the blockchain network, the network layer maintains the peer-to-peer network infrastructure. This layer is distinct from OSI network layers that include TCP/IP and other network protocols.

Consensus Layer

This layer outlines the rules for how nodes in the network reach an agreement on the blockchain's state, determining which transactions are valid and can be added. Different blockchains employ various consensus mechanisms, such as proof of work (Bitcoin), proof of stake (Ethereum 2.0), and delegated proof of stake (EOS).

Storage Layer

Here, blockchain data—blocks, transactions, smart contracts, etc.—is stored. Each full node in the blockchain network keeps a complete copy of the blockchain.

Middleware or Interface Layer

Comprising APIs, SDKs, and other tools, this layer enables developers to interact with the blockchain. It facilitates the development of decentralized applications (DApps) and services.

Application Layer (Layer 2)

This layer includes applications and services built on the Protocol layer. This encompasses decentralized finance (DeFi) applications, games, NFT marketplaces, and scaling solutions like the Lightning Network for Bitcoin or Plasma and Rollups for Ethereum.

Each layer serves a specific purpose and offers avenues for innovation and development. The versatility of these layers contributes to the power and adaptability of blockchain technology.

Often referenced are "Layer 1" and "Layer 2," analogous to "railroad vs. train" or "federal highways vs. local streets." Layer 1 provides the infrastructure, while Layer 2 builds upon it, optimizing the use of Layer 1 and potentially even constituting a different blockchain.

OSI Model's 7 Layers

The Open Systems Interconnection model (OSI model) is a conceptual framework that standardizes the functions of a communication or telecommunication system into seven categories, called layers. This helps different systems and software to communicate with each other.

1. Physical Layer (Layer 1)

This is the lowest layer of the OSI model. It's concerned with the physical characteristics of the communication medium (cables, connectors etc.), the transmission of raw bit stream over the medium, and the network equipment such as hubs and repeaters.

2. Data Link Layer (Layer 2)

This layer is responsible for node-to-node data transfer and error handling. It provides functional and procedural means to transfer data between network entities and to detect errors that may occur in the physical layer.

3. Network Layer (Layer 3)

The network layer controls subnet operations and is responsible for routing packets across potentially multiple networks and providing a consistent addressing scheme. Devices like routers operate at this layer.

4. Transport Layer (Layer 4)

The transport layer is responsible for transferring data between systems and hosts. It provides reliable, transparent transfer of data using error detection and correction. It also manages data packets by sequencing, and acknowledging packets of data. The most common transport layer protocols are Transmission Control Protocol (TCP) and User Datagram Protocol (UDP).

5. Session Layer (Layer 5)

The session layer establishes, maintains, and synchronizes the interaction between communicating systems. It organizes, synchronizes, and manages sessions between end-user application processes.

6. Presentation Layer (Layer 6)

The presentation layer ensures that the data is in a readable format for the application layer. It translates data from a format used by the application layer into a common format at the sender's end, then translates the common format to a format known to the application at the receiver's end.

7. Application Layer (Layer 7)

The application layer is the OSI layer closest to the end user, which means that both the OSI application layer and the user interact directly with the software application. This layer interacts with software applications that implement a communicating component. Examples of application layer protocols include HTTP (for web browsing), SMTP (for email), and FTP (for file transfer).

This is how networking works. The OSI model helps in understanding the whole network process, which makes network diagnosis, troubleshooting, and network enhancement easier.

So when you hear "this is a layer 2 switch," it means this switch understands and processes up to Level 2 of the OSI model. The dumber the device, the faster it can operate, but the less it knows about what it's transferring.

Here's a simplified list of network devices and their corresponding OSI layers:

1. **Hubs and Repeaters**: Physical Layer (Layer 1)

   These devices operate on the physical layer and are used for connecting segments of a network. They transmit the bits across the network without any filtering or routing.

2. **Network Interface Cards (NICs)**: Physical Layer (Layer 1) and Data Link Layer (Layer 2)

   NICs provide the hardware interface between a computer and a network. They can operate at both the physical and data link layer of the OSI model.

3. **Bridges**: Data Link Layer (Layer 2)

   Bridges connect two different networks at the data link layer, forwarding traffic based on the MAC address.

4. **Switches**: Data Link Layer (Layer 2)

   Network switches operate at the data link layer. They use MAC addresses to forward data to the correct destination.

5. **Wireless Access Points**: Data Link Layer (Layer 2) and Physical Layer (Layer 1)

   These devices provide wireless capability to a wired network. They operate on both the physical and data link layers.

6. **Routers**: Network Layer (Layer 3)

   Routers connect two or more networks and route packets among them based on their IP addresses. They operate at the network layer.

7. **Firewalls**: Network Layer (Layer 3), Transport Layer (Layer 4), and Application Layer (Layer 7)

Firewalls can operate on multiple layers. Traditional firewalls typically function at the network layer, but modern firewalls can function at the transport and application layers, providing more advanced controls. The higher the level, the better they can protect you.

8. **Load Balancers**: Transport Layer (Layer 4) and Application Layer (Layer 7)

   Load balancers distribute network traffic across multiple servers to ensure no single server becomes overwhelmed. Depending on their design, they can function at both the transport and application layers.

9. **Proxy Servers**: Application Layer (Layer 7)

   Proxy servers act as intermediaries for requests from clients seeking resources from other servers. They operate at the application layer.

10. **Gateways**: All Layers

   Gateways work at all layers of the OSI model. They act as the entry and exit point of a network, converting protocols among networks.

These are idealized categorizations, and the precise behavior can depend on the specific device and its configuration.

Chapter 4: It's Blockchain Time!

Evaluating Blockchains

Now that you're familiar with blockchain basics, it's time to evaluate its fit for your organization's unique needs and challenges.

Understand Your Needs: What issues are you addressing? Do you need a more secure way to store data? Do you need to streamline processes that require a lot of paperwork or multiple approvals? Perhaps you're developing a new product or service that needs a secure, transparent infrastructure. What are your expectations for network distribution, performance, and data storage? Do you need public read and/or write access?

Find the Match: Evaluate existing blockchains that can meet your criteria. Contrast your needs with market offerings. Some blockchains provide full source code, while others are only service-based.

Consider Costs and Benefits: Assess the trade-offs. Implementing blockchain may be costly and technically demanding. However, if the benefits—like increased security and long-term cost savings—outweigh these downsides, investment could be justified.

Trial and Error: Consider starting with a small-scale pilot project to understand blockchain's utility for your business without significant commitment.

The Blockchain Trilemma

Blockchains exhibit three key attributes often in tension:

1. **Security**: Essential for blockchain systems, security ensures tamper-proof and immutable records. Blockchain networks employ cryptographic algorithms, consensus mechanisms, and decentralized validation for data and transaction integrity.
2. **Scalability & Performance**: Scalability enables a blockchain network to manage increased transactions or users without sacrificing performance. As user volume grows, efficient transaction processing and low latency become critical. Assuming more miners will naturally join is naive and overlooks other bottlenecks.
3. **Decentralization**: A cornerstone of blockchain, decentralization eliminates central authority, distributing control among network participants. It fosters transparency, censorship resistance, and resilience against single points of failure.

The blockchain trilemma suggests that optimizing one attribute often diminishes the others. For instance, improving scalability might necessitate security or decentralization compromises, like employing off-chain solutions or sharding. Conversely, boosting security could slow down transactions or increase resource demands, while prioritizing decentralization may compromise performance and scalability.

Projects often navigate this trilemma based on their unique needs. Some prioritize security and decentralization over scalability, while others focus on scalability at the expense of decentralization. Various consensus algorithms, designs, and tech innovations aim to find optimal trade-offs.

Common trilemma solutions focus on prioritizing two attributes while compromising on the third. Security and decentralization are generally favored over performance.

Claims that a blockchain has "solved" the trilemma should be scrutinized.As an advisor to the news site CoinDesk, I have flagged many potential scammers making dubious assertions of achieving unprecedented speed without addressing this fundamental challenge.

A true solution will be headline news, warranting updates to this discourse.

The Infamous 51% Attack

The 51% attack exploits a potential vulnerability in blockchain networks when a single entity or coalition controls over 50% of the network's mining hashrate.

In a decentralized blockchain, miners validate transactions by solving complex math problems. The first solver adds a new block to the blockchain and receives a reward, in a process known as proof of work.

In a robust network, control is diversified among miners, preventing any single entity from manipulating the blockchain. However, with more than half the computational power, an entity could disrupt the network by:

- **Double Spend**: The entity could spend the same coins twice. After initiating a transaction, they could create a private chain without that transaction. If this chain overtakes the main chain, the original transaction is nullified.

- **Censorship**: The entity could block specific transactions, effectively censoring users.

- **Blockchain Reorganization**: They could alter the blockchain's history by mining a longer, secret chain and releasing it, causing nodes to adopt their chain version.

Though a 51% attack is theoretically possible, it's unlikely in large, diverse networks due to the computational and financial resources required. Smaller networks are more vulnerable.

Recently, miners have been pooling resources to stabilize income, effectively creating supercomputers from interconnected miners. This consolidation reduces the miner count and potentially makes blockchains more susceptible to attacks.

Private vs. Public Blockchains

You'll need to decide early whether to run your blockchain publicly or privately.

Public Blockchains
Public blockchains are open, decentralized networks. Benefits of public blockchains include:

- **Open Participation**: Anyone can validate transactions, create blocks, and earn rewards.

- **Transparency**: All transactions are public and anyone can audit the blockchain.

- **Security**: Maintained by a large network, enhancing security.

- **Decentralization**: Highly resistant to censorship due to lack of central authority.

Drawbacks include scalability challenges and reduced transaction privacy.

Private Blockchains
Also known as permissioned blockchains, these are open only to specific members and often used internally by businesses.

- **Restricted Access**: Limited to authorized users, making it more efficient but less decentralized.

- **Privacy**: Transactions are confidential within the network.

- **Scalability**: Typically faster and more scalable due to fewer participants.

- **Regulation**: Easier to comply with regulations due to centralized control.

Drawbacks include lower security and vulnerability to censorship.

The best choice depends on the specific needs of your organization or project. Public blockchains are more suitable for applications requiring transparency and resistance to censorship, while private blockchains are better suited for applications requiring privacy, speed, and regulatory compliance.

Interoperability

The terms *connected* and *disconnected* describe the interaction between various blockchain networks, relating to the concepts of *interoperability* and *isolation*.

Connected Blockchains (Interoperable)

Connected or interoperable blockchains can communicate and exchange information. They can read and understand transactions from other chains, allowing for seamless integration and interaction between different blockchain networks.

Benefits:

- **Cross-Chain Transactions**: Connected blockchains enable assets to be moved across different blockchain networks. For example, a digital asset on Ethereum could be moved to Binance's BNB Chain.

- **Enhanced Functionality**: By communicating with each other, different blockchains can leverage the capabilities and strengths of other networks.
- **Flexibility**: Users can take advantage of the benefits offered by multiple networks.

Disconnected Blockchains (Isolated)

Disconnected or isolated blockchains cannot communicate or interact with other networks. They operate independently and do not recognize transactions from other blockchains.

Benefits:

- **Security**: Disconnected blockchains can have a higher degree of security as they are less exposed to potential vulnerabilities from other chains.
- **Control**: Disconnected blockchains may offer more control over operation and governance, as they are not influenced by external networks.
- **Simplicity**: The lack of cross-chain considerations allows for simplified design and operation.

The industry is moving toward greater interoperability. Numerous projects aim to enable seamless cross-chain transactions, a key factor for blockchain adoption.

For bank-like entities wanting control and privacy, a private, closed blockchain is suitable. Most others will opt for a public, open blockchain.

Key Factors Checklist

When considering the potential benefits and risks of blockchain adoption, there are several key factors to consider. Be prepared to speak on these whenever promoting a blockchain solution to stakeholders or when writing white papers.

1. Business Needs and Goals: Start by understanding your business needs and goals. Is there a clear problem or inefficiency that blockchain technology could solve? Does blockchain align with your business strategy? Understanding these aspects is fundamental to any decision about blockchain adoption.

2. Cost vs. Benefit: Implementing a blockchain solution involves costs, including development, maintenance, and potentially high energy usage. Weigh these costs against the potential benefits such as increased efficiency, enhanced security, and reduced fraud.

3. Scalability: While blockchains can offer significant benefits in terms of security and trust, they can also struggle with scalability. In other words, as more nodes join the network, the time needed to process transactions can increase, slowing down the system.

4. Interoperability: It's essential to consider whether the blockchain system can interact with your existing IT infrastructure or other blockchain systems. If not, this limitation could require additional investment to integrate systems.

5. Security and Privacy: While blockchain is known for its high level of security, no system is entirely immune to attacks. Moreover, the transparent nature of blockchain may not be suitable for all applications, especially those requiring high levels of data privacy.

6. Regulatory Environment: The regulatory environment for blockchain is evolving. Depending on the industry and application, adopting blockchain could entail regulatory risks. It's important to understand and plan for these potential challenges.

7. Skill Availability: Implementing and maintaining a blockchain system requires specialized skills. If you lack these skills in-house, you'll need to hire or train staff, or outsource this work, which can be costly and time-consuming.

8. Change Management: Adopting blockchain often involves significant changes to business processes. This transition requires a well-planned and effectively executed change management strategy.

9. Long-term Viability: It's important to consider the long-term viability of the blockchain platform you choose. Is the platform well-supported and widely adopted? Does it have a strong community behind it? If the platform closes shop, is the source code open or held in escrow with your lawyer?

By carefully considering these factors, you can make a more informed decision about whether blockchain is right for your organization. It's also worth noting that a pilot project can be a good way to explore the potential benefits and challenges of blockchain without making a full-scale commitment.

Implementation Strategies

As a business leader, you must understand the key steps involved in implementing a blockchain successfully.

How to Write Your Own Blockchain

Don't!

It's akin to writing your own database. In other words, it's a complex process requiring a team and money.

If you've got the team and the money, it can be done, but consider yourself warned.

First: Are you sure your needs cannot be met by an existing blockchain?

If you want to create one that's "just like ___, but different," you may be able to modify the existing blockchain, or suggest improvements to the blockchain's developers.

Implementing a new blockchain from scratch involves numerous steps. It requires a deep understanding of blockchain principles and strong technical capabilities. Here are the key steps involved.

1. Define Your Blockchain Use Case

What problem will your blockchain solve? How will it provide value? Understanding this is critical to the success of your project. If your use case doesn't offer a benefit over existing blockchains, gaining traction will be more challenging. People in the security space strongly prefer verified solutions to unverified ones.

2. Design Your Blockchain

This includes decisions such as:

- **Blockchain Type**: Will it be a public or private blockchain? Will it be permissionless (anyone can participate in consensus) or permissioned (only certain nodes can participate in consensus)?
- **Consensus Mechanism**: How will your blockchain reach agreement among all nodes? Common mechanisms include proof of work, proof of stake, or other alternatives.
- **Blockchain Parameters**: What will be the block size and block time? How will the blockchain handle rewards?

3. Develop Your Blockchain

This typically involves:

- Developing the underlying blockchain protocol. This could be done from scratch, or by forking an existing blockchain.
- Setting up your nodes and blockchain network.
- Developing the consensus mechanism.
- Developing smart contract functionality, if applicable.

4. Test Your Blockchain

Testing is crucial to ensure the security and efficiency of your blockchain. You'll need to stress-test the network under different conditions, audit your code for potential vulnerabilities, and make sure all functionalities are working as intended.

5. Deploy Your Blockchain

Once your blockchain has been thoroughly tested, it's time to launch. This might involve mining the genesis block (the first block) and inviting nodes to join your network.

6. Maintain and Update Your Blockchain

Once your blockchain is live, it's important to continually monitor and maintain the network to address any issues or bugs that might arise. You'll also need to periodically update your blockchain to add new features or improvements. Make sure you put controls in place to allow for maintenance and updates before you go live.

Remember, these steps are high level and simplified. Implementing a new blockchain is a significant project requiring a broad range of skills, including cryptography, software development, and systems architecture. Careful planning and project management are also essential to ensure effective coordination of all implementation aspects.

How to Implement an Existing Chain

Implementing a blockchain project using an existing chain—also known as a blockchain platform or protocol—is a common approach that offers significant benefits, including reduced complexity, increased speed to market, and access to existing infrastructure and community. Here are the key steps involved:

1. Define Your Blockchain Use Case

Similar to building a blockchain from scratch, you need to understand and clearly define your project's objectives. What problem will your project solve? What are your performance and security requirements? What user needs must your solution meet?

2. Choose Your Blockchain Platform

Select a blockchain platform that fits your needs. Consider the platform's scalability, security, consensus mechanism, community support, development language compatibility, and whether it's public or private. Examples include Ethereum (good for smart contracts), Hyperledger Fabric (suitable for enterprise), or Binance's BNB Chain (low transaction fees) (If the name seems unfamiliar: Binance Chain and Binance Smart Chain merged to become BNB Chain in 2022).

3. Design Your Application

Design your blockchain application, also known as a decentralized application (DApp). This includes defining your data structure, user interface, and how your DApp will interact with the blockchain.

4. Develop Smart Contracts

If applicable, develop smart contracts to automate certain actions on the blockchain. These are self-executing contracts with the terms of the agreement directly written into code.

5. Test Your Application and Smart Contracts

Testing is crucial. This includes functional testing, smart contract testing, and performance testing. Security audits are particularly important for smart contracts, as once deployed, they cannot be changed. At this step many firms will hire security firms to review their contracts for security flaws.

6. Deploy Your Application

Once you're confident in the performance and security of your application, it's time to deploy. This may include deploying your smart contracts to the blockchain and your application to a suitable hosting environment.

7. Monitor and Update Your Application

After deployment, continue to monitor your application's performance and security. Collect user feedback and make necessary updates and enhancements.

8. Engage the Community

Particularly for public blockchains, community engagement is crucial. This could include everything from user support to governance participation.

Keep in mind, while using an existing blockchain platform reduces the complexity of dealing with lower-level blockchain protocol, it still requires a deep understanding of blockchain principles and the chosen platform, as well as strong software development skills.

Market Your Blockchain

If you build it, will they come? Not if they don't know about it. Whether you are inside an organization or trying to launch a new public chain, you will need to spend as much effort and money, or more, on marketing as you did on the chain itself.

Promotional Events: Gather your organization and teams to educate them about the new product.

Train Your Evangelists: Assemble a group of people who will focus on attracting interested parties to join your blockchain, whether through email, chat networks, or billboards. Create a grassroots movement. Developing a community is a crucial element in many successful projects.

Media: Reach out to internal or external publications to help disseminate your message.

Partnerships: Forming collaborations and partnerships with successful blockchain initiatives is often invaluable. These partnerships serve not only marketing purposes but also offer valuable early feedback, allowing for adjustments before it's too late.

Marketing Team: Assemble a marketing team tasked with popularizing your product. Provide them with both a budget and access to developers and evangelists.

Build a Good Team

Building a blockchain project requires a diverse set of skills, from understanding the underlying blockchain principles to applying them to practical applications. Here is a list of skills and qualifications you might look for when recruiting talent for your blockchain project. Not all of these need to be present in each candidate, but all should be covered by your team.

1. Understanding of Blockchain Fundamentals

An understanding of the underlying principles of blockchain technology is crucial. This includes concepts like

decentralization, consensus mechanisms, cryptography, smart contracts, and tokenomics.

2. Experience With Blockchain Platforms

Practical experience with blockchain platforms like Ethereum, Bitcoin, Hyperledger Fabric, or others is important. The person should know how to interact with these blockchains and their respective features.

3. Smart Contract Development

If your project involves the use of smart contracts, knowledge of Solidity (for Ethereum), Rust, or other relevant languages is crucial. They should also understand how to write secure and efficient contracts.

4. Cryptography

A background in cryptography can be very useful, as it's a fundamental aspect of blockchain technology. This includes understanding of public-key cryptography, hash functions, and digital signatures.

5. Programming Skills

Strong programming skills are a must. This might include languages like Python, Java, JavaScript, C++, or Go. The specific languages will depend on your project's requirements.

6. Back-End Development

Experience with back-end development can be particularly useful for developing the server side of your application, especially when integrating with a blockchain.

7. Database Management

Even though blockchain technology can act as a form of database, traditional database skills are still important for handling off-chain data.

8. Network Security

Given the high-stakes nature of many blockchain projects, a DevOps person with a background in network security can be very beneficial.

9. Decentralized Finance (DeFi)

If your project is finance-related, a solid understanding of DeFi principles, protocols and standards, as well as the areas of finance you'll be working with, is important.

10. Project Management

Lastly, the ability to manage a project, with skills such as coordination, time management, and communication, is essential for keeping the project on track. Consider agile methodology or other project management methodologies.

In addition to these technical skills, consider a candidate's passion for blockchain technology and their ability to work in a rapidly evolving field. Strong problem-solving skills and a lifelong learning mindset are highly valued in the blockchain space.

Risk Management

Any project or endeavor is bound to have some risks associated. Some are minor, some are not. It is a good idea to be aware of these early in the project so one can work it into the solutions being created, instead of the usual way of retrofitting them later, which leads to inferior results.

The way to do it is to assemble these documents and share them within the C level team. Each of these documents will have specific elements tailored to the unique needs and context of the organization, but generally, they all include identification of key resources, assignment of responsibilities, detailed procedures, and communication strategies.

1. **Contingency Plans**: These outline specific strategies and actions to deal with specific potential business disruptions. They usually include steps to maintain operational effectiveness in the face of events like natural disasters, technical failures, or supply chain interruptions.
2. **Risk Management Plans**: These focus on identifying potential risks in business operations and detailing strategies to mitigate these risks. They often include risk assessment, risk prioritization, and strategies for risk avoidance, reduction, or transfer.
3. **Business Continuity Plans (BCP)**: BCPs are designed to ensure the continuous operation of business functions during and after critical incidents. They include plans for maintaining essential functions and services in the event of disruptions like cyber attacks, power outages, or significant personnel loss.
4. **Disaster Recovery Plans (DRP)**: DRPs are a subset of BCPs, focusing specifically on the recovery of IT systems and data after disasters. They usually detail backup procedures, recovery site locations, and data restoration processes.
5. **Emergency Response Plans**: These are immediate action plans for responding to emergencies such as fires, natural disasters, or workplace accidents. They typically include evacuation procedures, emergency contact numbers, and first-aid processes.
6. **Crisis Management Plans**: These plans are designed to help organizations deal with significant adverse events. They focus on maintaining the organization's reputation and stakeholder communication during crises like scandals, legal troubles, or severe financial losses.
7. **Succession Plans**: Succession planning documents focus on the process for transitioning key roles within the organization. They typically include information on potential internal candidates, training programs, and transition timelines for critical positions.
8. **Backup Plans**: Generally, these are more informal plans detailing alternative courses of action if the primary plan fails. They can apply to various aspects of business, from project management to strategic decision-making.
9. **Incident Response Plans**: Focused on immediate response to security incidents, these plans outline steps for addressing and mitigating the impact of security breaches, such as cyber attacks or data leaks. They often include notification procedures, roles and responsibilities, and steps for containing and eradicating threats.

10. **Mitigation Plans**: These are developed to reduce or eliminate risks identified in the risk assessment phase. They cover a wide range of strategies, from implementing safety measures to diversifying investment portfolios, depending on the nature of the risk.

The list above is a good starting point, but there are more types of documents and plans that businesses might create to handle contingencies and unforeseen events. So you can research each type and see what, if anything, would be necessary for your business. For example here are some types of just the Contingency Plans:

1. Operational Contingency Plans
2. Financial Contingency Plans
3. Legal Contingency Plans
4. IT Contingency Plans
5. Human Resources Contingency Plans
6. Supply Chain Contingency Plans
7. Product Development Contingency Plans
8. Marketing Contingency Plans
9. Environmental Contingency Plans
10. Global or Geopolitical Contingency Plans

Why do this?

Beyond ensuring business continuity, risk management serves several other important goals. Each of these goals contributes to the overall resilience and long-term success of a business, beyond just the immediate objective of continuing operations during and after a crisis.

1. **Legal Compliance**: Many contingency plans, especially in industries like finance, healthcare, and manufacturing, are designed to meet legal and regulatory requirements. Failure to have adequate plans can lead to legal penalties and non-compliance issues.
2. **Risk Reduction**: By anticipating potential problems and setting out solutions in advance, these plans significantly reduce the overall risk to the business. This includes minimizing financial losses, protecting assets, and safeguarding employee well-being.
3. **Stakeholder Confidence**: While the first instinct may be to hide risks from investors and shareholders - the opposite is actually the best way to gain their trust and respect. Well-developed contingency plans can enhance the confidence of stakeholders, including investors, customers, and employees, in the organization's ability to manage crises effectively.
4. **Reputation Management**: In times of crisis, an effective response can help maintain or even enhance a company's reputation. Conversely, poor handling of a situation can lead to reputational damage. The smaller the space - the harder the reputation damage hits.
5. **Resource Optimization**: Contingency plans help in the efficient allocation and utilization of resources during emergencies, ensuring that critical functions have the necessary support while non-essential operations can be scaled back.
6. **Rapid Recovery**: These plans are designed to enable faster recovery from disruptions, thus reducing downtime and the associated costs.
7. **Operational Efficiency**: In some cases, the process of developing contingency plans can lead to the identification of operational inefficiencies, leading to improvements in normal business operations.

8. **Employee Safety and Well-being**: Particularly in industries with physical risks, contingency plans are crucial for ensuring employee safety in emergencies like fires, natural disasters, or health crises.
9. **Market Positioning**: Effective contingency planning can also provide a competitive advantage, as businesses that recover quickly from setbacks can capitalize on opportunities while competitors are still regrouping.
10. **Innovation and Flexibility**: Developing contingency plans can foster a culture of innovation and flexibility within the organization, as it encourages thinking about alternative strategies and solutions.

The effectiveness of contingency plans hinges critically on their availability and implementability (the ease and effectiveness with which a plan can be put into action). A contingency plan, no matter how meticulously crafted, is only as good as its implementation in a real-world scenario.

Blockchain-Specific Risks

Launching a blockchain product involves several uncertainties; it's important to have contingency plans in place to address potential issues. Address these early. Document all procedures and make them available to your team for when issues arise. Work through these procedures during the development stage to put the necessary plans in place. Here are some key contingencies to consider:

1. Security Breaches and Hacks: Despite blockchain's security benefits, breaches and hacks can still occur. Have a plan in place to detect and mitigate potential attacks. This plan could involve regular security audits, setting up alerts for suspicious activities, and having an incident response plan.

2. Smart Contract Failures: Once deployed, smart contracts can't be changed, making any bugs or errors potentially disastrous. Plan for regular audits of your smart contracts and consider implementing a multi-signature contract pause or kill switch for emergencies. Some chains allow for upgradable contracts through a specific interface; explore this option if your business cannot tolerate redeployment of a contract that changes its address.

3. Blockchain Forks: Forks in the blockchain can disrupt your project. Monitor the blockchain on which your project is built and have a plan for both soft and hard forks. This plan could involve supporting multiple chains or migrating to a different chain if necessary. Kill switches can be useful here as well.

4. Regulatory Changes: The regulatory environment for blockchain is rapidly evolving. Retain legal advisors to monitor any regulatory changes that could impact your project and plan for possible scenarios.

5. Technology Failures: Infrastructure failures, such as server downtime or loss of internet connectivity, can impact your project. Implement backup servers or a failover system. Regular backups and disaster recovery plans are also vital.

6. Market Volatility: If your project has a native token or interacts with volatile cryptocurrencies, market fluctuations could affect its viability. Develop strategies to manage this volatility.

7. User Errors: Users may lose access to their private keys, send transactions to the wrong address, or encounter other issues. Implement a support system to assist users, understanding that some errors may be beyond your control due to the immutable nature of the blockchain.

8. Network Scaling Issues: If your project succeeds, it may face scaling issues, particularly if it's built on a blockchain with limited capacity. Consider Layer 2 solutions or alternative blockchains to address potential scaling problems.

This is not a complete list. But

While planning for contingencies is essential, the evolving nature of blockchain technology means that unexpected challenges will arise. Cultivate a culture of adaptability and continuous learning to navigate these challenges effectively.

Blockchain Governance

Governance is a critical component of any blockchain network, especially in decentralized ones where decision-making power isn't held by a single authority. In essence, governance defines the rules for how proposals are made, debated, and implemented within a blockchain network.

There are several governance models and frameworks used in decentralized blockchain networks:

On-chain Governance: Rules for instituting changes are encoded into the blockchain protocol. Decisions are made through the mechanisms of the blockchain itself, usually by a voting process where the weight of a participant's vote might depend on the amount of tokens they hold or have staked (proof of stake). Examples include the DAOs in the Ethereum ecosystem.

Off-chain Governance: This is a more traditional approach, where decisions are made by a limited group of individuals or organizations, such as developers, miners, or a foundation associated with the project. While this can be more efficient, it can also be criticized as being less decentralized. Bitcoin primarily uses this model.

Consortium Model: In this model, a group of organizations or businesses control the consensus process of the blockchain. While this model is more centralized, it is practical for many business use cases where trust among participants is already established. Hyperledger Fabric is an example.

Some that are less known:

Futarchy: This is a more experimental form of governance, proposed by economist Robin Hanson. In a futarchy, prediction markets are used to gauge the potential impact of a decision, and the decision expected to most increase the value of the system is implemented.

Liquid Democracy: This is a hybrid model that combines aspects of direct democracy and representative democracy. Participants can vote directly on proposals, or they can delegate their voting power to a trusted party who votes on their behalf.

Council and Technical Committee: The decentralized Polkadot blockchain uses a multi-tiered system involving a council elected by token holders, a technical committee composed of teams actively building on Polkadot, and the general token-holding public.

Holacracy: This model aims to distribute authority throughout an organization rather than centralizing it. Each role in a holacracy is defined around the work that needs to be done rather than the people doing it. This model is less common in blockchain but could potentially be applied to DAOs.

Merkle Trees and Quadratic Voting: Ethereum's Vitalik Buterin proposed this model as a method of preventing collusion among voters in a DAO. Each user gets a number of votes (the square root of the total), and they can allocate these votes to various proposals. The number of votes allocated to each proposal is squared to determine the final weight of the votes.

Token Curated Registries (TCRs): This model allows token holders to curate lists on the blockchain. A TCR incentivizes token holders to curate the list's contents judiciously. This model could be used for a variety of purposes in a decentralized network, such as listing reputable service providers and quality digital assets.

SourceCred: This model assigns scores, called cred, to contributors based on their contributions to a project. This model aims to create a more equitable distribution of rewards within open-source projects.

Governance Minimization: This model advocates for minimizing the amount of on-chain governance as much as possible. The idea is to reduce the number of decisions that need to be made collectively to a bare minimum, hence reducing the chances of disputes.

Different networks require different governance structures, and the "best" model depends on a multitude of factors including the nature of the network, the degree of desired decentralization, and the type of decisions that need to be made. The key is to find the governance model that best aligns with the goals, participants, and use cases of your specific blockchain project. The model should also be able to evolve as the project and the wider blockchain ecosystem matures.

Chapter 5: Overcoming Regulatory and Legal Challenges

Blockchain projects can run into various regulatory and legal issues. Here are a few ways this can occur:

Securities Regulations: If a blockchain project involves issuing tokens or cryptocurrencies that could be classified as securities (like stocks or bonds), it can face regulatory scrutiny. In many jurisdictions, such as the United States, securities must be registered with regulatory bodies (e.g., the Securities and Exchange Commission).

KYC/AML Laws: Many countries have stringent Know Your Customer (KYC) and Anti-Money Laundering (AML) laws that require businesses to verify the identity of their customers and monitor transactions for suspicious activity. Blockchain projects, especially those dealing with cryptocurrencies, can potentially be used for money laundering or other illicit activities due to their pseudo-anonymous nature, and this can create legal complications.

Data Privacy and Protection: With regulations like the European Union's General Data Protection Regulation (GDPR) and similar regulations like the California Consumer Privacy Act or CCPA in the U.S., businesses must be careful about how they handle user data. Blockchains are inherently transparent and immutable, which can conflict with these regulations. A major concern is storing unprotected Personal Identifiable Information (PII), which includes any data that could potentially identify a specific individual. Any information that can be used to distinguish one person from another and can be used for de-anonymizing anonymous data can be considered PII.

Consumer Protection: There's a risk of fraud and scams in the cryptocurrency space, which can attract the attention of consumer protection agencies. Projects need to ensure they don't mislead consumers about potential returns or the security of their investment.

Cross-Border Transactions: The international nature of blockchain can pose a problem as different countries have different regulations. What might be legal in one country could be illegal in another.

Taxation: Tax authorities around the world are still figuring out how to deal with cryptocurrencies and blockchain technology. The unclear tax implications can cause compliance issues for blockchain projects.

Intellectual Property: As with any technology, issues around patents and copyrights can arise in blockchain projects. Determining who owns what part of a decentralized system can be challenging.

Smart Contract Legality: The legal status of smart contracts is uncertain in many jurisdictions. In some places, there might be issues related to the enforceability of smart contracts, especially when disputes arise.

Jurisdictional Issues: Due to the decentralized nature of blockchain, determining the jurisdiction for legal purposes can be complex. A dispute could arise in one country, but the nodes validating the transactions could be located in various countries around the world.

Cryptocurrency Mining Regulations: In certain regions, cryptocurrency mining could be seen as an energy-intensive process and could fall under environmental regulations.

Property Ownership: As blockchain begins to be used for recording property ownership and other legal rights, there may be conflicts between the blockchain records and traditional legal systems.

Supply Chain Regulations: When used in supply chain, it's crucial that the blockchain complies with local regulations related to product safety, standards, and imports/exports.

Insurance Regulation: If a blockchain project is used to underwrite insurance policies, it may be subject to insurance regulations which vary greatly from one jurisdiction to another.

Healthcare Compliance: Blockchain applications in healthcare must comply with laws and regulations such as the Health Insurance Portability and Accountability Act (HIPAA) in the U.S., which protects sensitive patient health information.

Financial Regulations: If a blockchain project involves financial transactions or services, it might need to comply with regulations governing banks and other financial institutions. In some jurisdictions, this could include regulations on capital requirements, payment processing, and fraud prevention.

Future Regulation: Blockchain regulation is often behind, which may be exploited for profit. Businesses can look at lists of unfair practices in comparative industries and implement them to get an edge in an unregulated space. Beware: This is a surefire way to get regulatory disapproval and make your business a target of investigation. It also means that when regulations change, your business will be required to make those changes or close.

These are just a few of the potential legal and regulatory issues. It's always important to consult with legal experts when embarking on a blockchain project.

Do Your Homework!

Overcoming the regulatory and legal challenges of implementing blockchain technology can be a complex process, but here are some key steps to consider:

Understand the Regulations: One of the first steps is to gain a thorough understanding of the laws and regulations that apply to your project in every jurisdiction where you plan to operate. This includes not only blockchain and cryptocurrency-specific

regulations, but also laws related to your specific industry or application. For instance, a healthcare-related blockchain project would need to comply with health information privacy laws.

Consult With Legal Experts: Legal advice from lawyers who are knowledgeable about both blockchain technology and the relevant regulatory landscape is invaluable. They can help you navigate the regulatory intricacies and provide advice on the best course of action.

Engage Regulators: Early and proactive engagement with regulatory bodies can help clarify expectations and avoid misunderstandings. Providing regulators with information about your project and its benefits can help build a positive relationship. In some cases, regulators may be able to provide guidance or exemptions for innovative projects.

Incorporate Compliance Into Design: Where possible, incorporate regulatory compliance requirements into the design of your project from the outset. For instance, if you need to comply with KYC laws, make sure your system has a way of verifying user identities.

Be Transparent: Transparency about your project, its aims, and its operations can help build trust with regulators, users, and the public. It can also reduce the risk of misunderstandings or suspicion.

Plan for Change: The regulatory environment for blockchain is still evolving, so it's crucial to stay up to date with changes and be prepared to adjust your project accordingly. This can mean regularly reviewing your compliance strategies and being prepared to pivot if necessary.

Join Industry Groups: Blockchain and cryptocurrency industry groups often engage in lobbying and advocacy to shape regulations in a way that is favorable to the industry. They can also provide resources and advice on regulatory compliance.

Regulatory Sandbox: Some jurisdictions have introduced the concept of a "regulatory sandbox," which is a framework that allows innovators to conduct live experiments in a controlled environment under a regulator's supervision. Such environments can help in understanding how a particular blockchain-based service might operate under current laws and regulations.

Privacy Enhancing Technologies (PETs): Incorporating PETs like zero-knowledge proofs and secure multi-party computation can allow blockchain solutions to stay compliant with data privacy regulations.

Standards and Certifications: Following industry standards and achieving relevant certifications can be helpful in demonstrating compliance efforts. For instance, the ISO/TC 307 standard is being developed for blockchain and distributed ledger technologies.

Build Flexible Systems: Given the fluid nature of the regulatory landscape, designing systems with the ability to be updated or adapted is crucial. For instance, being able to modify your blockchain's privacy settings will allow you to respond to changes in data protection regulations.

Cross-Border Cooperation: Collaborating with entities in different jurisdictions can help to navigate international regulations. This is particularly relevant for blockchains since they are inherently borderless.

Education and Advocacy: Educating policymakers and regulators about blockchain technology can lead to more informed regulatory decisions. It also helps to actively advocate for favorable policies and regulations.

Internal Governance: Implementing strong internal governance structures can help ensure ongoing compliance and risk management.

Remember, every blockchain project is unique, so the specific steps needed to overcome regulatory and legal challenges will vary. Consulting with legal experts is crucial to ensure that you're fully compliant with all relevant laws and regulations.

How to Get Out of Trouble

If you get into hot water with a regulator, ignorance is a poor defense. "But Firm X did it too" is unlikely to help either: Firm X may have done things differently, or it may have been served with the same papers yesterday!

Your best bet is to show documentation of due diligence performed prior to a potential problem. Providing evidence that you acted in good faith increases the chance that the regulator will make a decision in your favor and help you come into compliance. Do your homework before launch, adjust your strategy to stay compliant and do the best you can. And document, document, document. If someone is unhappy, the ability to "show your work" can make a huge difference.

If a regulatory agency or other authority has expressed a concern or disapproval related to your blockchain project, it's important to act quickly, professionally, and transparently. Here are some steps you can take:

Verify the Source: There have been cases where "concerned citizens" have taken it upon themselves to create letters that range from "cease and desist" to "boy, you are in trouble!" Always verify notices before reacting to them.

Acknowledge and Respond Promptly: It's important to respond quickly to any communication from regulatory authorities, to show respect for their role and to avoid exacerbating any problems through delay. Done properly, this can also verify the source.

Engage Legal Counsel: If you don't already have lawyers specializing in blockchain and your industry area, now's the time to engage them. They can provide advice on your response strategy and may also help you communicate with the agency.

Understand the Issue: Seek to fully understand the concern or issue the agency has raised. If necessary, request clarification from them.

Review Internal Processes: Check your internal processes (this is why it's important to have those in place beforehand) to see if they were correctly followed and if they may need to be improved to avoid similar issues in the future.

Prepare Your Case: With your legal team, prepare your response. This should include any facts, arguments, or explanations that will help to address the agency's concerns.

Cooperate Fully: Demonstrating a willingness to cooperate can go a long way in resolving disputes or issues. If you're asked for more information, provide it promptly and thoroughly.

Be Transparent and Proactive: Inform your stakeholders about the situation and your approach to resolving it. This may include customers, investors, partners, and staff.

Learn and Adapt: Use the experience as a learning opportunity. Update your practices and procedures to prevent a similar situation in the future.

Negotiation and Mediation: If there is room for discussion, consider negotiation or mediation to come to an agreement. This can be particularly useful when there's a gray area in regulations or when the regulation has never been applied to a technology like blockchain before.

Compliance Audit: Conduct a thorough compliance audit to identify potential areas of non-compliance beyond the ones pointed out by the agency. It's better to proactively address all possible issues to avoid further regulatory scrutiny in the future.

Training and Education: Ensure that all relevant staff members are trained on regulatory requirements and internal compliance procedures. Sometimes, a regulatory issue can arise from a simple mistake or misunderstanding that could be avoided with better training.

Public Relations Strategy: It might be beneficial to prepare a public relations strategy to handle any media attention or public backlash that could occur as a result of the agency's dissatisfaction.

Regulatory Technology (RegTech): Consider implementing RegTech solutions, which are technological tools designed to facilitate compliance with regulations more efficiently and effectively.

Consider Repercussions on Partnerships and Relationships: Any regulatory issue may affect your relationships with other stakeholders, such as partners, customers, and even your bank. Be prepared to address their concerns and potentially review contracts or agreements if necessary.

Revision of Business Model: If regulatory compliance can't be achieved with the current business model, it might be necessary to consider revising the model itself. While this is a big step, it's better than facing legal consequences.

Remember, it's crucial to respect the role of regulatory agencies and to work cooperatively with them, even when disputes arise. Their goal is to protect consumers and the integrity of the financial system, which ultimately benefits everyone. Getting mad or being disrespectful never solved any misunderstandings. Be ready, be prepared, document everything.

Avoid Problems Before They Start

Navigating regulatory and legal challenges can be tricky, but there are strategies to help mitigate potential problems. Many of these apply to traditional finance as well. (Some of these are repeated from earlier lists, for completeness).

Geographic Location: Select your company's location based on favorable and clear regulations related to blockchain. Some countries are more progressive and have clear guidelines, which can be advantageous. Just be aware that your potential customers know that, too, and projects from lenient jurisdictions come with a lower reputation baked in.

Avoid or Limit Usage of Tokens: Tokens often bring additional regulatory scrutiny because they can sometimes be classified as securities. If your blockchain project can operate without a token or with limited usage of tokens, this might help avoid some potential issues.

Collaborate With Regulators: A proactive approach can be beneficial. This means working with regulatory bodies from the outset to ensure that your business model and operations comply with all necessary rules and regulations.

Seek Legal Counsel Early: Engage a legal team that has expertise in blockchain technology and the regulations that govern it in your chosen location. This can help you identify potential regulatory and legal hurdles before they become a problem.

Stay Informed: Regulations in the blockchain space can change quickly. Stay up to date on any changes to ensure your project remains compliant.

Adopt Transparency: Transparent operations can help you gain the trust of regulators and stakeholders, making it easier to work through any potential issues.

Understand and Respect KYC/AML Laws: Know Your Customer (KYC) and Anti-Money Laundering (AML) laws are an important part of financial regulations globally. Even if you don't deal with tokens or cryptocurrency, respecting these laws can avoid unnecessary scrutiny.

Be Cautious with Marketing Claims: Overpromising or misleading investors and customers can attract regulatory attention and potentially lead to legal challenges.

Implement a Strong Compliance Program: A strong internal compliance program can catch potential issues before they become regulatory or legal problems.

Consider Traditional Business Models: Where possible, consider applying traditional business models that regulators are more familiar with. This could make it easier for them to understand and approve your operations.

Outsource Regulatory Compliance: For some businesses, it may be more efficient to outsource compliance to third-party companies that specialize in regulatory affairs in the blockchain space. These firms have a thorough understanding of various jurisdictions and can provide a roadmap for compliance.

Partnerships With Banks and Traditional Financial Institutions: Partnering with established financial institutions can lend credibility and regulatory experience to your project. These institutions are familiar with the regulatory landscape and can often provide guidance.

Avoid Controversial Applications: Some blockchain applications, such as gambling or adult content, are likely to attract more regulatory scrutiny. If possible, it's best to avoid such applications.

Apply for Regulatory Sandbox: Some jurisdictions offer a "regulatory sandbox"—a controlled environment in which businesses can test innovative products under the regulator's supervision. This can help you understand how your product fits within the regulatory framework.

Plan for Regulatory Changes: Laws and regulations can change, often quite quickly. By planning for potential changes, you can mitigate the impact of sudden regulatory shifts.

Self-Regulatory Organizations (SROs): Joining or creating an SRO can be beneficial. SROs can lobby on behalf of their members, provide self-imposed rules and guidelines, and often have a better line of communication with regulatory agencies.

Educate Regulators: Often, regulators are playing catch-up with new technologies. By openly communicating with them and educating them about your business and blockchain technology, you can help shape the regulatory environment.

Remember, while these strategies can help, it's impossible to avoid all regulatory and legal risks when operating in the blockchain space. The goal should always be to minimize risk and operate in a transparent, compliant manner.

Chapter 6: Blockchain Security and Privacy

Balancing privacy and transparency is one of the key challenges when it comes to blockchain technology. On one hand, blockchain's ability to offer a transparent and immutable ledger can improve trust and reduce fraud. On the other, the need for privacy, especially when dealing with sensitive data, is paramount. Let's talk about these issues a bit more:

Transparency: The transparency of blockchain comes from its open nature, where each transaction is recorded and can be viewed by all participants in the network. This transparency can increase trust and accountability because it's nearly impossible to alter past transactions without the consensus of the network. This feature makes blockchain particularly useful for applications like supply chain management or auditing, where tracking the history of transactions is important.

Confidentiality: Despite the transparency, maintaining confidentiality on blockchain is crucial, especially in industries dealing with sensitive data like finance or healthcare. Raw transaction data on a blockchain could reveal sensitive business or personal information. Therefore, blockchains must be designed in a way that protects this data.

Balancing these two aspects involves several techniques:

Zero-Knowledge Proofs: Zero-knowledge proofs allow one party to prove to another that they know a value, without conveying any information apart from the fact that they know the value. This is used in blockchain to verify transactions without revealing underlying details.

Private and Public Keys: Blockchain uses public key cryptography. Each user has a pair of keys—a public key that is openly shared and a private key that is kept secret. Anyone can encrypt a message using a public key, but only the person with the corresponding private key can decrypt it.

Permissioned Blockchains: Unlike public blockchains, permissioned blockchains restrict who can join the network and what transactions they can see. This allows them to maintain confidentiality while still using a decentralized ledger.

Off-Chain Transactions: Sensitive data can be stored off-chain, and only hashes or references to the data can be stored on the blockchain. This can ensure data privacy while still providing the benefits of an immutable ledger.

Ring Signatures: Ring signatures are a type of cryptographic signature that can be performed by any member of a group of users, each having keys. Any resulting signature cannot be linked back to a single user, thereby maintaining the privacy of the individual who initiated the transaction. This is used in cryptocurrencies like Monero to maintain transaction privacy.

Homomorphic Encryption: This is a method of encryption that allows computations to be carried out on ciphertext, thus generating an encrypted result which, when decrypted, matches the result of operations performed on the plaintext. This allows for privacy-preserving computations and transactions.

State Channels: State channels are "second layer" solutions that allow users to interact with each other off-chain, only settling the final state of their interactions on-chain. This can significantly improve privacy because the details of the interactions are only known to the participants.

Mimblewimble: This is a blockchain format where there are no addresses and the data storage required is minimized. This helps to improve both scalability and privacy.

Plasma: Similar to state channels, Plasma is a framework for scalable off-chain transactions. It allows for the creation of "child" blockchains tied to the parent Ethereum blockchain. Transactions can occur on these side-chains with the security of the main chain, preserving privacy and reducing transaction load on the main chain.

Sharding: Sharding is a scaling solution that breaks a database down into smaller pieces, called shards, each of which can be processed independently of one another. In terms of privacy, sharding can help by reducing the amount of data that a single node needs to process, which reduces the chances of sensitive data being exposed.

Tumblers/Mixers: These are services that mix potentially identifiable or "tainted" cryptocurrency funds with others, making it harder to track the funds back to their original source and increasing privacy.

Personal Identifiable Information

Handling Personal Identifiable Information (PII) is a major consideration when developing blockchain projects, and it can present a regulatory and legal challenge. Blockchain's transparency and immutability do not mesh well with current data privacy regulations, most notably the General Data Protection Regulation (GDPR) in the European Union, which grants users a right to erasure, requiring that companies be able to "forget" users at their request.

PII includes any data that could potentially identify a specific individual. Any information that can be used to distinguish one person from another and can be used for de-anonymizing anonymous data can be considered PII.

The GDPR and other similar regulations (like the California Consumer Privacy Act or CCPA in the U.S.) mandate strict requirements on how companies can store and use PII. Violations can lead to hefty fines. Therefore, if your blockchain project involves storing or handling PII, you must incorporate strong data protection measures and have clear consent from users regarding data usage.

In many cases, it is best to avoid storing PII on the blockchain altogether. Instead, you could store references or hashes that can validate information stored off-chain, where it can be managed with more flexibility.

This is a complex issue and one that ideally should be reviewed with competent legal counsel to ensure your project complies with all relevant regulations while still delivering its intended value proposition.

While information can be protected from tampering, it's crucial to think in advance about how to protect your users from exposure or from revealing who owns what assets. Creative solutions are necessary. For instance, if everyone knows that your biggest investor is Bob and you issue account statements without names, it will become obvious not only which account is Bob's but also what other assets he holds outside your project. Therefore, consider subdividing accounts or employing other strategies to allow for auditing without making concrete information readily available when it's not in the best interest of your users.

Security Highlights

Privacy can be compromised if your security isn't being enforced properly. Securing blockchain-based systems and protecting sensitive data is essential. Blockchain itself comes with inherent security features like decentralization, cryptography, and immutability, but those alone aren't sufficient. Best practices for enhancing security include:

Private Keys: Private keys should be secured meticulously. If a private key is lost, the assets associated with it are also lost. If it's stolen, those assets can be stolen. Key management solutions or hardware security modules can be used for this purpose.

Multisignature Wallets: For added security, consider using multisignature wallets (multisig). These require more than one private key to authorize a transaction, adding an additional layer of security.

Regular Updates: Always keep the blockchain software up to date. Updates often include patches for security vulnerabilities.

Use Permissioned Blockchains When Needed: If the information is very sensitive, consider using a permissioned blockchain, which allows only designated participants to validate block transactions.

Use Secure Coding Practices: As with any software system, ensure that secure coding practices are followed. Regular audits and code reviews can help detect and eliminate potential vulnerabilities.

Node Security: Secure the nodes in the network by limiting the exposure of your network endpoints, applying network segmentation, and protecting the node with traditional IT security measures like firewalls and IDS/IPS.

Limit Data Stored on the Blockchain: Avoid storing sensitive data directly on the blockchain. Instead, consider storing a hash of the data or a reference to the data stored in a secure off-chain database.

Smart Contract Auditing: Smart contracts, being self-executing pieces of code, can contain vulnerabilities. It is important to thoroughly audit the smart contract code and test it before deployment.

Employ Identity and Access Management (IAM): Implement robust IAM solutions to ensure only authorized individuals can access and perform transactions within the network.

Education and Training: Blockchain users should be educated about phishing threats, secure passwords, and other basic cybersecurity practices. This is often overlooked but can be crucial in preventing security breaches.

While blockchain has inherent security features, it's not impervious to attacks or errors. Good security practices and regular audits are important to maintain the integrity and security of a blockchain-based system.

Chapter 7: Hand-in-Hand Tech

Many modern technologies can integrate with blockchains to create powerful, secure, and innovative applications. Keeping an eye on these may help you start a new business in a new subsector. Here are a few examples:

Internet of Things (IoT): IoT devices generate vast amounts of data. Blockchain can provide secure, immutable storage and enable device-to-device transactions in a decentralized IoT network. Blockchain can also boost security for IoT devices. IoT devices can also act as oracles and executors for smart contracts.

Artificial Intelligence (AI): Blockchain can make AI models more transparent and explainable. AI can improve the efficiency of blockchain networks by making mining or consensus algorithms more effective. AI can also act as quality control for smart contracts and other code.

Big Data and Analytics: Blockchain can improve the reliability, traceability, and security of collected data, making it more valuable for analytics. In turn, analytics can be used to extract valuable insights from blockchain data.

Near Field Communication (NFC): Blockchain can add a layer of security to NFC transactions, making them more secure and reliable. This could be particularly useful in applications like contactless payments or secure access control. A lot of progress has been made in recent years, but vast new levels of integration have been left unexplored. New NFC tags with encryption became available recently, bridging the gap in security with earlier NFC chips.

Virtual and Augmented Reality (VR/AR): Blockchain could be used to manage virtual assets, identities, and transactions in VR/AR environments.

5G Networks: 5G is set to increase the amount of data being transferred between devices. Blockchain can help manage and secure this data, as well as enable new business models, like decentralized network infrastructure.

Robotics and Automation: Blockchain can facilitate secure, trustless machine-to-machine communication and transactions, essential in automated systems.

Cybersecurity: Blockchain's inherent properties like decentralization, immutability, and cryptography significantly enhance data integrity and security, which can be leveraged for various cybersecurity applications. For example, if routers demanded new firmware be encrypted, signed and only available through a blockchain, fewer would be owned by hackers.

Cloud Computing & Edge Computing: Blockchain can be used to create decentralized cloud storage solutions, enhancing security and reducing reliance on single providers. In edge computing scenarios, it can facilitate data processing and decision making at the edge of the network, enhancing privacy and reducing latency.

The implementation and effectiveness of these integrations can greatly depend on the specific use case and design of the blockchain itself. We will discuss some of these topics further in the Emerging Trends section.

Chapter 8: The Future of Blockchain

Blockchain technology is continually evolving, and with this evolution comes new trends and advancements. Here are things to watch out for:

Interoperability: The ability of blockchain networks to communicate and interact with each other. Interoperability will allow for cross-chain transactions and enhance the overall utility and efficiency of blockchain networks. Standardization of cross-chain protocols will be the key to moving this forward.

Scalability Solutions: Technologies like Layer 2 solutions, sharding, and sidechains are being developed to increase transaction speed and volume. This can address one of the biggest challenges in blockchain: scaling up to meet demand.

Decentralized Finance (DeFi): DeFi is revolutionizing the financial industry by offering decentralized alternatives to traditional financial systems and services. It's likely to continue growing and innovating. New solutions appear on a regular basis. This is one of the hottest new things in Fintech already and it will be for years to come.

Central Bank Digital Currencies (CBDCs): Many central banks are researching or developing their own digital currencies. These could provide the benefits of blockchain technology while maintaining the stability and trust associated with central banks. Governments will likely strengthen regulations around blockchains before releasing their currencies into the wild. Contracts will be highly regulated and controlled centrally.

Non-Fungible Tokens (NFTs): These unique tokens represent ownership of a specific item or piece of content and are becoming popular in the digital art and collectibles markets. The world is full of items, and items have owners. The world is full of venues, and venues need proof of access. Ownership is one of the key aspects of society, so expect to see numerous new uses for NFTs.

Privacy Enhancements: New techniques, such as zero-knowledge proofs and homomorphic encryption, are being developed to improve privacy and security on the blockchain. This will enable greater separation between users and their data, allowing for better privacy and access control.

Enterprise Blockchain: Companies across industries are adopting blockchain for its transparency, security, and efficiency benefits. This trend is expected to continue as more use cases are discovered. Other companies are releasing blockchains as a service. Not every company is equipped to run their own blockchains, so this is a welcome addition that should increase adoption while decreasing horror stories of data breaches resulting from companies in over their heads. Collaborations, like R3, have proliferated despite built-in conflicts of interest. The best solutions are the ones that the market decides on, so we are likely to see more stand-alone products and services.

Blockchain and IoT: Integrating blockchain with the Internet of Things (IoT) can increase security, enable better tracking of devices and products, and improve overall efficiency.

The rise of connected devices generates a vast amount of data and requires robust security to prevent breaches. The integration of blockchain in IoT ecosystems can enable secure, verifiable, and automatic exchanges of data or services, leading to entirely new business models.

From oracles to monitoring to execution, IoT has a bright future with blockchains. But blockchains can help IoT just as much. The vast majority of existing IoT widgets don't utilize encryption or blockchains, which results in vulnerability. They are known "backdoors" for hackers. Embracing blockchains and encryption is sure to make a huge difference for IoT.

Blockchain and AI: Combining blockchain and artificial intelligence can enhance data security, improve decision-making, and enable new business models. Perhaps we can use blockchains to keep AI in check, avoiding the doomsday predictions cropping up around this emerging technology.

AI could provide advanced analytics for blockchain data, enhancing decision-making and efficiency. It can also help in automating complex tasks and security measures within blockchain networks.

Regulation and Compliance Technologies: As blockchain becomes more mainstream, the need for regulatory compliance tools will grow. These technologies can help ensure that blockchain transactions comply with local and international laws.

5G Technology: Running nodes on a busy blockchain can result in quite a bit of traffic. The increased speed and decreased latency of 5G could improve the efficiency of blockchain networks, making it feasible for applications requiring real-time data, such as autonomous vehicles or real-time supply chain tracking. As 5G coverage gets wider, the ability to run nodes on all sorts of devices (phones, IoTs) in the field becomes more realistic, adding to the spectrum of problems that blockchains can help with.

Quantum Computing: This is a double-edged sword. On one hand, quantum computers could break the cryptographic systems protecting current blockchains, posing a significant security risk. On the other, the development of quantum-resistant cryptographic algorithms and quantum blockchains could usher in a new era of security and speed. Popular blockchains have already been patched for vulnerabilities that quantum computers create by their mere existence.

Augmented Reality (AR) and Virtual Reality (VR): Blockchain may provide the infrastructure for verifying and trading in-game currencies and other virtual assets, contributing to the growing field of virtual economies.

Edge Computing: The foundational principle of edge computing is enhancing efficiency and performance by bringing data storage and computation closer to the locations where they're needed, effectively reducing latency. In conjunction, it enhances decentralization by distributing computational resources away from a central hub. When we integrate these benefits with blockchain technology, we experience a substantial uplift in security, courtesy of advanced encryption methods. Simultaneously, blockchain's inherent qualities of data integrity and the versatility of smart contracts are introduced into the system. Together, these two technologies can revolutionize processes, making them more streamlined, secure, and efficient.

Data Privacy Regulations: The global trend toward stricter data privacy regulation, like GDPR in Europe, could affect the design and operation of blockchain networks, particularly those that store personal data. Blockchain networks could be utilized as a benchmark or framework for establishing regulatory requirements in other systems, particularly in the context of private data encryption, permissioning and handling of keys. In simpler terms, the qualities and standards set by blockchain networks for handling data privacy could be used as a model or guideline for how other systems (not necessarily blockchain-based) should manage and protect personal data to comply with regulations like the GDPR.

And there could be new issues, unseen before: A system is required to purge personal data upon request. Someone writes a list of personal info into a blockchain as plain text. There are no tools to deal with such data exposure on a public chain. How would regulators respond?

Decentralized Identity (DID) Solutions: With the growth of digital platforms, managing digital identities securely and efficiently is becoming crucial. Blockchain can play a key role in the development of DID solutions, providing a secure, decentralized infrastructure for managing digital identities. A number of countries have replaced systems similar to U.S. Social Security numbers with encrypted solutions. The next logical step is to move digital identities to a blockchain.

Cloud Technology: The continued advancement of cloud platforms is likely to increase the accessibility of blockchain-as-a-service solutions, making blockchain technology more approachable for smaller businesses and organizations. Amazon already offers Amazon Managed Blockchain, and Google Cloud provides its Blockchain Node Engine. Many more companies are expected to follow suit.

The development and adoption of these technologies will depend on several factors, including the regulatory environment, societal acceptance, economic feasibility, and technological advancements.

The Future of Digital Wallets

The wallets of today are undergoing significant changes and are becoming more than just simple key storage. In the era of Web 3.0, blockchain wallets are envisioned to become user-centric digital identity hubs, facilitating seamless interaction with decentralized applications (DApps) and various blockchain platforms. Here's how this is taking shape:

Integrated DApp Browsers: Many modern wallets have integrated DApp browsers. These allow users to directly interact with Web 3.0 applications without leaving their wallets. Users can browse DApps just like they would with a regular web browser, but with added functionality, including seamless transactions and interactions with smart contracts.

Cross-Chain Compatibility: Wallets are increasingly becoming chain-agnostic, meaning they are designed to work with multiple blockchains. This simplifies asset management for users who would otherwise need to use a different wallet for each blockchain. This cross-chain compatibility also extends to DApps built on different blockchains.

Better User Interfaces (UI): Wallets are also focusing on improving user experience. This includes more intuitive UIs that make navigation easier for non-tech-savvy users. The aim is to make transacting and interacting with DApps as simple and straightforward as using a regular web app.

Integration of DeFi Services: Many wallets are integrating DeFi services directly into their interfaces. This gives users the ability to lend, borrow, stake, swap tokens, and more, right from their wallet, without needing to interact with different platforms separately. It also gives wallet creators a direct path to collect fees from transactions from third-party integration partners.

Identity and Data Management: Wallets are also becoming tools for managing digital identities and personal data. Users can manage their online identities, verify credentials, and control how their personal information is shared across Web 3.0 platforms.

Enhanced Security Features: As wallets become more central to the user's interaction with the digital world, their security features also evolve. Biometric authentication, hardware wallet integration, multi-signature support, and secure key recovery mechanisms are all being incorporated.

Overall, the trend is toward making wallets a seamless gateway to the world of blockchain and Web 3.0, providing a unified, secure, and intuitive interface between users and the decentralized web. If the companies behind traditional browsers aren't careful, they may get left behind.

Chapter 9: Starting a Business

About 1 in 5 U.S. businesses fail within their first year of operation, according to the U.S. Bureau of Labor Statistics (BLS). After five years, the failure rate is up to half. With 5 million businesses started each year in the U.S., that means 2.5 million will not succeed.

Coincidentally, marriage success rates are also around 50%. But people keep starting both, so we need to learn how to do it right.

We are not going to go through each step; there are better books for that. But let's discuss what you need to know about starting a blockchain business.

From Idea to Success Story

Starting a business involves numerous steps, and the journey from an idea to a functioning business can be quite involved. Here is a high-level overview of the process:

Ideation: Think about what you're passionate about and brainstorm business ideas related to that. Research the market, understand potential competitors, and figure out how you can differentiate your offering.

Market Research: Conduct comprehensive market research to understand your target audience, their needs and preferences, the competition, and market trends.

Business Plan: Develop a detailed business plan outlining your vision, mission, goals, target audience, marketing and sales strategies, revenue model, and financial projections.

Find Your Niche: Based on your market research, narrow down your business focus to a particular niche where you can offer something unique and valuable.

Validation: Validate your business idea through methods such as surveys, focus groups, or a minimum viable product (MVP).

Legal Structure: Decide on a business structure (sole proprietorship, partnership, corporation, LLC) and register your business with the relevant government body.

Brand Identity: Create your brand identity, which includes your business name, logo, and tagline. Ensure these elements align with your brand message and appeal to your target audience.

Funding: Determine your funding needs. You may need to pitch to investors, apply for loans, or bootstrap using your own resources.

Marketing and Sales Strategy: Develop a strategy for how you will reach your target audience and convert them into customers. This could involve social media marketing, content marketing, SEO, paid advertising and public relations.

Product Development: Based on your validation and feedback, develop your product or service. This could involve manufacturing, programming, content creation, or any other form of product development depending on your business type.

Website and Online Presence: Develop a professional website and establish your presence on social media and other relevant online platforms.

Launch: Launch your product or service. This may involve a launch event, promotional offers, press releases, influencer collaborations, or other marketing activities.

Operations and Customer Service: Set up your operations, logistics, and customer service processes. These should be geared toward meeting customer needs effectively and efficiently.

Continuous Improvement: After the launch, continuously monitor your business performance through metrics and customer feedback. Use these insights to improve your product, marketing, customer service, and other aspects of your business.

Growth and Scaling: Once you've established your business and started making a profit, consider strategies for growth and scaling. This could involve expanding your product line, entering new markets, or automating and outsourcing tasks.

The path from idea to functioning business is never a straight line, and it requires a lot of hard work, flexibility, and resilience. But with determination and the right strategy, you can turn your business dream into a reality.

Ideation

So, that's all great academic knowledge, but how does one actually go from "I want to do something" to "I have an idea!"? Let's work through the steps.

Disclaimer: building a successful business requires more than ideas. And many successful firms have been started without having any ideas.

One way to germinate ideas is to look at "what's coming up": trends, regulations, volatility, market optimizations.

Let's cheat and look at the previous chapter "The Future of Blockchain" for inspiration. Let's pick a few:

Interoperability: The ability for different blockchain networks to communicate and interact with each other.

Scalability Solutions: Technologies like Layer 2 solutions, sharding, and sidechains are being developed to increase transaction speed and volume.

Central Bank Digital Currencies (CBDCs): Many central banks are researching or developing their own digital currencies.

So now that we know the topic and direction, we can apply them in Improvisational Brainstorming.

Improvisational Brainstorming

Here is a multi-phase approach to creative problem solving that I sometimes use. The process is akin to a brainstorming technique used in various creative fields, including theater. It's similar to the improvisational (improv) technique known as "Yes, And," where actors build on each other's ideas without negating or dismissing them. This encourages a free flow of ideas and fosters creativity. You can do it in a group or alone. I recommend doing it alone at first, to get a feel for the process before egos and negativity get in the way of understanding the technique. You will also appreciate the difficulty and respect others more for diving in with you.

Some practitioners from the arts and entertainment industry suggest various chemicals. I recommend doing this sober, as an altered mind leads one to connect concepts and ideas that should not be connected. And we are looking for tangible, useful ideas, not funny ones.

You are not always looking for crystal-clear business ideas here. Sometimes what you want to get out of the process are predictions on needs, services and trends, which you can then use to generate your business idea. This process can be repeated recursively. The further you go, the less likely your idea has been done already — but the more likely there is a reason why it hasn't.

Here's your guide:

Embracing the Unfiltered Creativity

In the journey of generating ideas, our first step is to establish an open, unjudging space where every thought, no matter how unconventional or dumb, is welcomed. This stage is not about filtering or evaluating; it's about allowing your mind to roam freely, much like actors in an improvisational theater who engage in the "Yes, And" technique. They accept every idea, building upon it, weaving a rich tapestry of creativity. Sometimes what seems dumb initially may be just a misunderstood or underdeveloped good idea.

The 'Yes, And' Philosophy

Imagine each idea as a stepping stone. The principle of "Yes, And" teaches us to not only acknowledge each idea (the "Yes" part) but to also expand upon it (the "And" part). This method fosters a cascade of thoughts, where one idea leads to another, pushing the boundaries of conventional thinking. It's a powerful tool for unlocking creativity, encouraging a brainstorming session where ideas flow without restraint.

Transitioning to Analysis and Refinement

Once this creative dump has been unleashed <u>and captured</u>, the next phase is to sift through the ideas, much like a gold miner panning for nuggets of gold. This stage is about critical thinking — analyzing, scrutinizing, and evaluating the ideas to extract those that are most promising and relevant. It's a process of distillation, finding the essence of practicality and innovation within the creative outpour.

Grounding Ideas in Reality

The final step in our journey is the verification and research phase. The ideas that have emerged as frontrunners now need to be tested against the touchstone of reality. This involves research, validation, and practical assessment to ensure that these ideas are not just creative but also viable and applicable. It's a crucial step that marries creativity with practicality, ensuring that the ideas can stand the test of real-world application. It's advisable to do some light risk management at this stage as well.

Practice Run

And now let's pontificate with great vigor and aplomb that:

CURRENT STATE OF BLOCKCHAIN

Today's blockchains were designed to be decentralized and free of authority. Mission achieved!

Ethereum, one of the most popular chains, has failed to keep up with demand and failed its clients and adopters. Its failure gave rise to a dozen lesser chains whose creators vowed to dedicate themselves to speed and lower cost of transactions, at any cost.

The battle for "The One True Chain" has ended. We ended up with:

- a bunch of disjointed, disassociated chains, each with a different set of capabilities and specialties.
- a few side-chain hangers-on, there to improve certain aspects of their parent chain, usually unusable by regular humans.
- a bunch of web and app wallets, full of different features, covering from one to a few blockchains. Most are unable to move assets themselves between all blockchains as well as subchains.

WHAT IF?

What if we generalize what's happening now and envision where that evolution would lead if applied to blockchains as a technology? This means ignoring the initial motivations, stigmas, players and their goals. Apply true "you are all welcome" rules to users, companies, blockchains and governments alike.

What it looks like to me is something of a bridge that connects them all in a smooth, cooperative manner. Allowing one chain to talk to them all. With assets moving smoothly across chains, without a need for a degree in cryptography and hours of YouTube and RTFM research.

THE SHORT ANSWER

The answer, I'm going to suggest, is that everyone runs a chain instead of just owning a wallet. And I do mean everyone.

A chain per person, per group, per company, per country.

However you imagine using wallets now, replace that with a chain-plus-wallet pair.

On each chain, a particular address could serve as a "box" for another
address on another chain, similar to how side chains operate now.

THE SETUP

We have the following players, generally speaking (I'll use same
throughout this document):

General population — your average person.

Companies that are users of these services.

Financial companies who will expand on-chain products and offer
assets. Banks, for example.

Governments that have fiat currencies and want to offer digital assets
and other certification and record services (CBDCs).

SIDE CHAINS

Let's examine how a typical side chain works. I will take some poetic
license and may generalize the main concepts:

Say we have a main chain. Let's say it's Ethereum based.

So say one party (**User1**) has a bunch of addresses combined into their
one software wallet, **EthWallet1**.

  EthAddress1 10 ETH, 50 USDT

  EthAddress2 5 ETH, 100 USDT

And say we have a side chain called **SideChain1**.

This usually means that the owners of **SideChain1** have created an
EthAddress3 that acts like an "IOU safe" or an escrow account. It
provides users with a mechanism by which an asset from **EthAddress1**
when moved to **EthAddress3** gets a mirror asset on **SideChain1** deposited
into an account that **User1** established as theirs inside **SideChain1**
(say **SideChain1-Adress5**).

If the two chains use the same account generation algorithm, one can play games such that **EthAddress1** and **SideChain1-Address5** would have the same ID and private key on both chains. Simply put, I go to my wallet software (like Metamask), switch network preference from Ethereum to Polygon and my same Account1 now shows me my assets inside Polygon.

Note that the chains don't all need to be Ethereum for this, just the algo used to generate the two keys. The algorithm doesn't even need a working blockchain to work, just the necessary math to maintain the protocol.

The process isn't smooth for the end user, and the degree of ugliness is highly dependent on which network and subnetwork we are talking about. Most side chains have huge warnings about loss of assets if "the dance" of transferring assets wasn't danced perfectly.

GLOBAL VISION: MAP THE WORLD WITH CHAINS

Knowing how side chains run, it's not hard to envision a world where there are millions of chains that belong to anyone. Where a particular person's address on one chain is tied to that person's address on another chain, and assets can move across them seamlessly, similar in concept to, say, a networking router mechanism.

So my **personal** chain is tied to my **bank**'s chain. And their chain is tied to the chain that is run by the government with jurisdiction over the bank.

The chains come with the trust that the owner of the chain holds.

People can issue new assets and services on their own chains, and such assets can be trusted based on the trust in their chain being authentic and truthful. I won't be trusted to issue a U.S. dollar, but I can probably be trusted to issue my own NFTs, records, or software.

People and companies can pick and choose the chains best for their regular needs, store data cheaply and effectively, and only interact with other chains when/as necessary.

This is the opposite of the current model, in which everyone is forced to use the same chain to where demand exceeds mining and technology resources. **It would hugely reduce demands on larger chains like Ethereum,** improving their effective speed and lowering their transaction costs.

People and companies can keep all their internal transactions and records safe, secure and private, and only use the shared addresses for public transactions or to transfer/convert some external assets to internal and vice versa.

Chains can restrict who has read/write/mining access. They can introduce "administrator" accounts that can fix mistakes or wipe out hacking attempts, if needed. No more lost assets due to lost keys, if that particular chain wants to support it. Admins would (obviously) only have admin access to their own chains.

People and companies can **transact with each other on their chains** (both chains would track the event and transaction records would be co-signed by both parties). Keeping transactions away from major chains will reduce their load, cut costs, and result in fewer bottlenecks.

Users should be able to create transactions across multiple chains to facilitate trusted transactions. Two parties that don't trust each other can create a transaction that uses their own trusted chains ("I'll use my bank's chain and you use your bank's chain"), that through a routing algorithm will figure out how the two banks will settle their transaction. They may do so directly, via other banks, or via a government-run chain, if they happen to use the same one.

FINALLY, A TRUSTED AUTHORITY

One of the benefits and the main selling point of a chain like Ethereum is the absence of a governing body that can reserve transactions.

That's all cool and awesome until someone gets hacked or a transaction with a side chain goes into limbo and assets are lost.

Currently there are no ways to handle this. No way to even freeze an account unless one had the foresight to set up a proper smart contract (most stable currencies support that, by the way).

By keeping your assets inside your bank's chain, one can always appeal to them to reverse or cancel a transaction. Banks can charge for arbitration, reversals, deposits/withdrawals etc. They can also be better at verification of the participants and destinations for transactions via AML/KYC.

GOVERNMENTS WELCOME

All governments would like to increase the use of their fiat. The wider it's used, the stronger the fiat is, and the more they can hide the money-printing to pay for projects. Avoiding the crypto world has created a gap, which "stablecoins" filled. Highly distrusted stablecoins are still popular. Imagine if actual USD was offered, backed by the actual Federal Reserve?

This leads me to believe that governments will finally stop fighting blockchains soon enough. They will now be motivated to run their own chains. They will simply want the benefits. As a positive side effect, people will benefit from the transparency this system offers. Government will want to offer their currency for easy conversion and use. The mechanisms for printing fiat on top of blockchain are not only easy, but can match how fiats are operated by a country. And the ease of printing or removing coin is extremely attractive. The ability to track where the money went for both, the government and the people of that country, is also extremely attractive.

The side effect is governments can now issue financial aid, welfare, medical payments in a special coin that can be properly tracked, can expire if desired, and can only be spent by the issuer and only with the correct party.

Exchanging, sending and donating money to other countries, banks, and entities will be no easier than a financial wire is today.

ACH will become faster, worldwide, and more reliable.

This should also solve the taxation problem. People will likely only transact in the fiat-derived coin with trusted chains run by financial companies, which would then report to government agencies or via the government chain directly.

To elaborate: If the government issues an asset on their chain, it can restrict who gets an account. It can demand transparency for account creation and may choose to only allow access from compliant chains, like banks. It will be able to see allocation of the asset across these bank accounts. It can demand, as a condition of having that account, to see or audit all sub-accounts of that bank. It can demand that the bank reports who holds this asset and disclose transactions on their chain in that asset. Taxes can be levied based on that information.

Anyone who decides to rely on untrusted chains to hide their money from taxes will run a risk of losing it all if that chain is compromised. They would also need to run multiple chains to avoid being spotted, making it more difficult to not get caught. Most people will likely comply and tie their chains to bank and government chains, for ease of use and reliability.

(UN)STABLECOINS

From the first stablecoin to the new algorithmic stablecoins, history is full of shady practices and shuttered accounts. In our new model, stablecoins are backed by governments and institutions that are audited by trusted government authorities. This would reduce the impact of uncontrolled stablecoins by reducing their supply as people switch to alternatives with higher authority, better transparency and proper auditing. Snowball schemes will be harder to pull off when the real underlying stablecoin backed by properly regulated entities is just as easy to get.

TO BLOCKCHAIN OR...

All of this will result in a need for a standard API from each blockchain (any blockchain that doesn't want to be left in the dust) to provide a consistent API that also includes support for merging addresses between blockchains. Kind of like the APIs Metamask relies on.

One can obviously create a non-blockchain system to expose the same API, but it's not trivial and they would need to put forth a lot of effort to do so. Larger firms and governments that have a lot of existing infrastructure may want to do so. But for most chains this will be risky as interoperability, long-term upgrade costs and security risks of custom software would make this an illogical choice. So I would expect open-source solutions here to lead in adoption.

HOW TO MAKE MONEY KNOWING THIS

These products and services will be of value:

Wallet systems that can support going cross-chain. Or wallets that can emulate a chain.

"Chain for rent" services. Certain chains can be used to create smaller chains, perfect for individual, group, or company use. Even traditionally written databases that can emulate a protocol similar to Ethereum's would work here.

Arbitration services could receive payment for arbitration between chains. This would require them to run nodes on these chains and support some sort of "he said/she said" backup/restore/compare protocols.

Backup/restore services. These will likely be provided by banks as these are easy to turn into financial and insurance products. And there is a huge benefit to having an authority for running such services. But someone will make money writing and selling them.

Rating agencies for chains.

Banks will want to be on the chains as well. One brings in USD to their bank. They charge a percentage to issue money to the chains.

Books on the subject.

Market Research

Now that we have ideas, we can cycle through them and determine which to move forward with. The first step, before we create our business plan, is market research.

Market research is a critical step for various reasons, especially for understanding your customers and your competition. Here's why:

Competitive Analysis: Market research helps you understand who your competitors are, what they offer, their strengths and weaknesses, and their strategies. This knowledge can help you differentiate your product or service and find your competitive edge. This also helps you price your product and see what others are making in that sector/industry/product line.

Understanding Customer Needs: Market research provides valuable insights into what your potential customers need and want, their preferences, buying habits, and the price they are willing to pay. This helps you tailor your product or service to meet these needs effectively as well as project future income.

Market Validation: Before launching a product or service, you need to know if there is a demand for it. Market research can validate your business idea by proving there's a market for what you're planning to offer.

Reducing Business Risks: By giving you a clear picture of the market conditions, market research can help you make informed decisions, reduce risks, and avoid costly mistakes.

Identifying Opportunities: Market research can uncover trends, gaps, and opportunities in the market that you can take advantage of to grow your business.

Planning Marketing Strategies: The information obtained from market research can guide your marketing strategies, helping you target the right audience in the right way and at the right time.

Improving Customer Satisfaction: By understanding your customers' needs and preferences, you can enhance your products, services, and customer service, leading to higher customer satisfaction and loyalty.

Overall, market research is a powerful tool that can increase the likelihood of your business success. It helps you make data-driven decisions and ensures that your strategies align with market realities.

Practicing Market Research

As we cycle through the ideas we generated above, throwing out the duds (too easy, too hard, not enough cowbell, etc), we get to the idea of starting a **rating agency**.

So our task is to become an expert in the industry or bring in talent that already is. Maybe even hire away or find a retired senior exec from competition. Good investors always look at who in the startup is actually an expert in the core product of the startup.

Competitive Analysis

We would look at the way rating agencies work now and try to understand their models.

- Who are the top competitors in this space?
  Moody's, Standard & Poor's, and Fitch.
- How do they make money?
  - **Issuer-Pay Model:** The most common revenue model for these agencies is the issuer-pay model, where the entity that issues the financial instruments (like bonds, debt securities) pays the rating agency to rate these instruments. This model is predominant because it allows investors to access the ratings for free, promoting widespread distribution and use of the ratings.
  - **Subscription Services:** These agencies also earn revenue by selling subscriptions to their research, detailed reports, and analysis. Investors, financial institutions, and other entities pay for these subscriptions to gain deeper insights into the creditworthiness of various entities and the risks associated with different investment opportunities.
- What sorts of products do they provide?
  - **Credit Ratings**: Assess the creditworthiness of corporations, countries, financial products.
  - **Risk Assessment and Analysis**: Tools and analytics for assessing and managing credit risk. Services for understanding and managing market risk exposure.
  - **Research and Reports**: Analysis and forecasts of economic and financial trends. In-depth analysis of various industries and sectors. Reports on specific topics, such as the impact of regulatory changes or emerging market trends.
  - **Data and Analytics**: Comprehensive financial data and analytics. Tools for comparing financial performance against peers or industry standards.
  - **Consulting and Advisory Services**: Management consulting type services. Tailored consulting services for specific client needs, such as risk management strategies and financial modeling. As well as educational services.
- Do any currently offer ratings for blockchains, blockchain firms or blockchain financial assets?
  - Moody's has issued ratings on some funds which issue their own ETFs via Ethereum and Stellar blockchains.

- o Rating companies can and do rate private companies. One can contact them for details.
    - o As this book ages - others will likely get into this space.As with any startup - timing matters.
- How hard would it be for the big competitors (Moody's, Standard & Poor's, and Fitch) to get into this niche?
    - o Could their models support it?
    - o What would be their roadblocks?
    - o Why haven't they done it yet?
    - o Are they likely to specialize on the blockchains, blockchain based assets or would they be better off covering product companies that utilize blockchains?
- What do they charge for similar services?
- Are there related products customers may want in association?
- What would be the client's expectations?
- What do competitors specifically make/lose money on, so we can avoid it?

Some of these can be answered by reading their sales brochures. Other things may require reading articles. Any firm that's public will publish their 10-Ks (annual reports). Reading one would give you exact details about their internal money flows, which departments are profitable, and lots of other useful information.

AI is a great research tool, but be aware that sometimes AI will make stuff up. So any insight you get from an AI - always check it externally. Or you'll be staking your company's future on a randomly formed pathway that has no basis in reality.

Understanding Customer Needs

To first understand your customer's needs - one must first understand who their customers are. It's not always cut and dry. For example with Social Media companies - the platform users think they are customers, but they are actually the product. While firms that buy ads and personal data are the actual customers. "Follow the money" - see who is paying you money - they are the true "customer", others are just "platform users".

To a rating agency, depending on the business model - the customers would be those who buy consulting services, pay for ratings to be formulated, or the people/companies that are using ratings themselves.

As with any company - now you can pay a group of potential customers to give you feedback on what they want, what they expect, and how they expect it to be assembled and presented to them, as well as rough costs.

I had the pleasure of knowing a math professor who used to do management consulting at one point in his career. Told me a story where a firm brought them in to analyze "what's wrong, from the outside". He took some of their customers to bars and they gave him all the info he needed to help the firm out. Be creative, assume people who do something for a living know what they are talking about.

Aside from the generic "business risk" which is covered in many books, when it comes to blockchain businesses - important differentiation is understanding regulatory trends and compliance requirements. It is crucial in the blockchain space, where legal frameworks are still developing. Market research assists in navigating these complexities, enabling businesses to mitigate legal and operational risks. By staying abreast of regional and global regulatory changes, companies can adapt their blockchain strategies accordingly, ensuring long-term sustainability and reducing the risk of legal challenges or operational disruptions. This strategic approach, grounded in thorough market research, is essential for businesses looking to leverage blockchain technology effectively while minimizing associated risks.

Having survived multiple "Crypto Winters" (where value of crypto falls, significantly reducing investment pools), I also recommend adhering to the risk of running out of money. Luckily a lot of people will work for coin or percentage in the company in this industry. Try to capitalize on it. Not all jobs need to be full time. Try to save the funds for payments you can't avoid. Build a basic version, find more funding, rinse and repeat.

Know when to kill a project. If you have a project that's not moving forward - you may be better off shutting it down and saving investors money. They will respect you for it and you may be more likely to have your next project funded.

For a marketing company: maybe assemble a group of analysts and marketers and offer them partial pay as a percentage of the firm or of the business they generate. Build a solid affiliate program system that people can trust.

Get a legal opinion on what you can and can't do as a firm, and build it into internal procedures.

Try to land investors who can help gain traction instead of just concentrating on the money.

Planning Marketing Strategies

Everyone seems to be an expert in marketing these days. We've all heard and read so many random articles - it seems nothing new is left to learn. But don't let that stop you from hiring a professional firm or two. I found there is a huge gap between professional marketers and self-developed ones. If you have it in the budget - spend the money.

Preferably get ones who know how to market to the crypto crowd, which can be a very different culture and require a different approach. Look at the list of your customers and customize to marketing talent familiar with those groups.

Improving Customer Satisfaction

The gradient of customers goes from people who wanna read nothing to people who will want to read tons of pages before they buy your product. And from "anything will do" to "must be delivered in silverlined boxes, with carriage, with entourage.

As a startup, do not fall into the track where each customer gets the same treatment. But do agree on standards you are willing to maintain for which tiers and products.

Try to figure out monetization angles across all tiers and products. Offer consulting engagements, training, speeches. All these will increase bottom revenue and establish trust with customers. A rating business is "in business of authority", so customer loyalty and satisfaction will depend on the firm establishing authority and maintaining it.

Business Plan

A business plan is a comprehensive document that outlines your business goals, the strategy you'll use to achieve them, the market in which you plan to operate, and financial projections. It's a crucial roadmap guiding the launch and growth of a new business and serves several critical purposes:

Attracts Investors and Lenders: Business plans are often necessary when seeking funding from investors or applying for a business loan. It shows potential stakeholders the viability of your business idea and your strategy to make it profitable. You need to educate them and convert them to your cause.

Guides Business Growth: A business plan sets out your business's direction, helping you make informed decisions as you start and grow your business. It needs to say things you can and will do to achieve market dominance. It also needs to cover things you will not do, to avoid confusion or false competition comparisons. A business that does "everything" is usually not perceived as a good investment.

Assists in Managing Cash Flow: The financial section of your business plan helps in budgeting and managing cash flow efficiently. It needs to explain where the money will go, to demonstrate sharp focus on deliverables and achieving marketing goals.

Helps Attract Partners or Team Members: A strong business plan can help attract partners and key employees by showcasing the potential and direction of the business. It can help them see themselves as valuable to the goals of the business.

Acts as a Feasibility Check: A business plan helps you verify that your business idea is viable, identify potential hurdles, and develop strategies to address them. Founders often wear blinders and this is a good place to verify the vision makes sense to others.

Here's what typically goes into a business plan:

1. Executive Summary: A brief overview of your business, including your mission statement, business structure, ownership, and a summary of your plans.

2. Company Description: Detailed information about your company, the problem it solves, the customers it serves, and its competitive advantages.

3. Market Analysis: Detailed research about your industry, target market, and competition.

4. Organization and Management Structure: Your business's organizational structure, details about the ownership, and information about your management team.

5. Products or Services: Information about what you're selling or the service you're providing.

6. Marketing and Sales Strategy: How you plan to market your business and attract customers, including your sales strategy.

7. Funding Request: If you're seeking funding, this section outlines your current funding requirements, future funding requirements over the next five years, how you will use the funds you receive, and the types of funding you are considering.

8. Financial Projections: This section provides an overview of your business's financial outlook, with forecasts for revenue (sales forecast), expenses (fixed costs like rent and salaries, variable costs like raw materials and shipping), cash flow statements, capital expenditure budget, and profitability projected over time.

9. Appendix: An optional section that includes additional supporting documents such as resumes, permits, leases, or contracts.

While these are the general sections of a business plan, they may vary based on your specific circumstances and the audience of your plan. Always customize your business plan to best serve your business's unique needs. Think of it like a battle plan: Here's what we are going to do and how we will do it!

Practicing a Business Plan

Note: This is a highly simplified example. Many more details would be needed in an actual business plan.

Executive Summary

Our business, *Blockchain Rating Solutions* (BRS), aims to provide an unbiased, comprehensive, and transparent rating system for blockchain networks. Given the exponential growth and evolving nature of the blockchain industry, BRS aims to empower investors, businesses, and individuals with credible, thoroughly researched, and unbiased information about various blockchains, contributing to safer and more informed decision-making in the industry.

Company Description

Blockchain Rating Solutions is a start-up poised to fill a critical need in the blockchain industry. Our goal is to be the industry standard for blockchain assessments, offering in-depth evaluation on aspects such as security, scalability, interoperability, decentralization, and legal compliance. We serve investors, financial institutions, tech companies, and individuals who require accurate and timely information to navigate the complex world of blockchain.

Market Analysis

As blockchain technologies continue to evolve and permeate various sectors, there is an increased demand for unbiased information and assessment. Currently there are only 1,000 blockchains operating in the world. We expect this number to be 1 billion in 10 years. With over 10,000 cryptocurrencies in existence and numerous other blockchain projects in various stages of development, the potential market for our services is vast and continuously growing.

Competitive analysis reveals a gap in the market for a dedicated blockchain rating agency. Most existing information sources are either too technical or too generic, failing to provide the nuanced, easy-to-understand evaluations required by our identified target audiences.

Organization and Management Structure

Blockchain Rating Solutions will be a limited liability company with three co-founders sharing equal ownership. We will be structured around four key departments: Research, Business Development, Marketing & Public Relations, and Finance & Administration. The Research department, our core, will consist of blockchain analysts, technology experts, and financial analysts.

Services

Our primary service will be providing ratings and reports on various blockchains. These ratings will be based on a comprehensive methodology evaluating factors like technology, security, governance, use cases, connectivity of the chains and assets allocated. We will also provide custom research services and risk assessment solutions for businesses exploring blockchain implementation.

Marketing and Sales Strategy

We plan to position ourselves as thought leaders in the industry through content marketing, webinars, and partnerships with tech media outlets. Our website will offer limited free content to attract visitors, while detailed reports and custom services will be behind a paywall. We will also focus on building relationships with strategic partners such as financial institutions, tech companies, and regulatory agencies.

Funding Request

We are seeking an initial investment of $2 million for operational setup, technology, market research, and marketing activities. These funds will provide the necessary capital to hire a proficient team, establish an online platform, and conduct initial blockchain evaluations.

Financial Projections

Given the potential market size and the innovative nature of our service, we anticipate rapid growth after the initial development stage. We project positive cash flow by the second year and expect to become profitable by the third year of operation. An Excel file with five-year projections for expenses, sales forecast and profits is attached with this proposal.

Appendix

Available upon request: Resumes of founders, Market research data, Sample rating reports.

Chapter 10: Founder's Exit Strategy

Another aspect of any new business that people often don't talk about early enough is the length and purpose of their involvement. Many think it's taboo to discuss, akin to dirty laundry. But one should do it and do it early.

The choice of exit strategy influences business decisions, including the business model, funding methods, and growth strategies. Different exit strategies can shape the company's culture and stakeholder expectations.

Given the volatile and innovative nature of blockchain and cryptocurrencies, exit strategies in this sector can be quite different from traditional businesses.

Common exit strategies include IPOs, ICOs/IEOs/IDOs, acquisitions by larger crypto entities, mergers with traditional financial institutions, or transitioning to a decentralized autonomous organization (DAO).

Each strategy necessitates a distinct set of goals, frameworks, and procedures. It's crucial for a company to align its early-stage decisions with its intended exit path.

For instance, a firm eyeing an initial public offering (IPO) must prioritize regulatory compliance, financial transparency, and robust corporate governance from the outset. Conversely, a blockchain startup contemplating an initial coin offering (ICO) should focus on developing a compelling token economy and ensuring technological robustness. Similarly, transitioning to a decentralized autonomous organization (DAO) requires embedding principles of decentralization and community governance into the company's DNA.

Failing to align these foundational elements with the chosen exit strategy can lead to significant challenges down the line, ranging from regulatory hurdles and investor distrust to operational inefficiencies and strategic misalignments. It's not just about selecting an exit strategy but systematically and strategically preparing for it from the very beginning.

IPO

In the realm of blockchain ventures, an initial public offering (IPO) represents a significant transition from a privately held entity to a publicly traded company. A cryptocurrency firm considering an IPO must develop an appropriate business and financial strategy from inception. The company must be built with a focus on regulatory compliance, transparency, and corporate governance, aligning with the stringent requirements of stock market regulators like the SEC in the U.S. Additionally, the firm must demonstrate a stable revenue model, clear growth potential, and robust financial health, often requiring a shift from a purely technology-driven approach to a balanced business strategy.

Executing an IPO involves substantial costs, including legal and accounting fees, underwriter expenses, and ongoing costs related to regulatory compliance and reporting. The process typically entails extensive audits, the creation of detailed financial reports, and navigating complex legal frameworks to ensure compliance with securities laws. These requirements often mean that the company has to invest significantly in legal and financial expertise, internal controls, and corporate restructuring.

In practice, a crypto firm's IPO journey begins with selecting underwriters, followed by drafting a prospectus detailing the company's financials, business model, and risk factors. This prospectus is then reviewed by regulators before the firm can embark on a roadshow to attract potential investors. The final step is the actual public offering, where shares are sold to investors on a stock exchange. This transition not only opens new avenues for capital but also subjects the company to greater public scrutiny and accountability, a stark contrast to the often opaque and fluid nature of early-stage crypto ventures.

Expect it to cost around $2 million on the low end due to compliance and legal expenses.

ICO / IEO / IDO

An initial coin offering (ICO) is a pivotal fundraising mechanism unique to the blockchain and cryptocurrency world, often used as a means for startups to bypass the rigorous and regulated capital-raising process required by venture capitalists or banks. In an ICO, a company creates and sells its own cryptocurrency token to raise capital, typically to fund the development of a new product or service within the blockchain ecosystem. This approach requires a different set of strategic considerations from traditional fundraising methods.

From the outset, a firm planning an ICO must focus on developing a compelling and technically sound blockchain project, as the value proposition of the ICO is directly tied to the potential utility and innovation of the project. This involves meticulous planning around the token's design, its integration into the project's ecosystem, and the underlying blockchain technology. The firm must also create a detailed whitepaper outlining the project's goals, technology, the mechanics of the ICO, and the token's utility.

The goal is to create a token that trades on a major exchange(s), much as a stock trades on a traditional exchange after an IPO.

The cost of conducting an ICO can vary significantly but generally includes expenses related to technology development, legal compliance, marketing, and security. Legal compliance is particularly crucial, as navigating the regulatory landscape of different countries can be complex. The company must ensure its ICO complies with securities laws and regulations regarding cryptocurrencies, which can differ widely across jurisdictions.

In the United States, for example, the SEC forbids the unregistered public offering of security tokens. For a discussion of the difference between security and utility tokens, see Chapter 2.

To get listed on a respectable exchange, it is important to prepare for the ICO correctly. Expect to spend over $1 million.

Here's an example of costs. These will change over the years and across exchanges:

What	How much
Listing fee	$300,000
Marketing	$200,000
Market-Making (MM)	$100,000

Equity Deposit/Liquidity Pool	$500,000

The liquidity pool deposit is posted directly to your distributed exchange and/or given to your market-making company. It is needed to continue to make a market for your coin after launch, ensuring sufficient liquidity for trading. This liquidity allows users to buy and sell the new token with less unexpected change in trade execution price, known as slippage. The liquidity pool needs to be "locked" alongside your minted coin for months. If your coin doesn't maintain its price over time, the pool may be depleted by the time you can get the deposit back.

Conducting an ICO also involves launching a marketing campaign to generate interest among potential investors, typically through social media, cryptocurrency forums, and other online platforms.

The actual sale of tokens is usually executed through smart contracts on a blockchain, ensuring transparency and security. Investors in an ICO typically receive digital tokens that can represent a stake in the project, a right to use the project's services, or speculative instruments betting on the future value of the project.

While ICOs can offer significant fundraising potential and lower barriers to entry compared with traditional methods, they also come with high risks for both the company and investors, including regulatory scrutiny, the potential for fraud, and high market volatility. A firm considering an ICO must balance these factors while maintaining a strong focus on innovation, regulatory compliance, and investor relations.

An initial exchange offering (IEO) and initial DEX offering (IDO) are variations on an ICO where the money for tokens is collected not by the company itself, as in an ICO, but by the exchange (in an IEO) or a distributed exchange (in an IDO).

With an IDO, one can save some money on listing fees, but there will be fewer people able to easily buy your coin. However, the popularity of decentralized exchanges (DEXes) could grow, so do your research when you are ready to conduct your offering.

DAO

A decentralized autonomous organization (DAO) represents a groundbreaking exit strategy in the blockchain space, fundamentally different from traditional approaches like IPOs or ICOs. A DAO is an organization represented by rules encoded as a computer program that is transparent, controlled by the organization members, and not influenced by a central government. This model is particularly appealing to blockchain-based firms due to its alignment with the principles of decentralization and community governance.

For a blockchain firm considering transitioning to a DAO, the process involves a fundamental reimagining of corporate structure and governance. From the beginning, the business must be built with decentralization at its core, focusing on community involvement and transparent, algorithmic decision-making. This means prioritizing the development of a robust, secure, and scalable smart contract infrastructure that can automate key aspects of the organization's operations and governance.

The financial direction for a DAO is unique as it often involves the issuance of tokens to its members, which represent voting power or a stake in the DAO. These tokens can be distributed through various means, such as an initial sale, rewards for contributions to the DAO, or even as part of a transition from an existing business structure.

In practice, creating a DAO involves several key steps:

1. **Developing the Smart Contract**: This is the backbone of the DAO, outlining the rules of operation and decision-making processes.
2. **Funding**: DAOs often require initial capital, which can be raised through token sales or contributions from founding members.
3. **Deployment**: The smart contract is deployed on a blockchain, making the DAO operational.
4. **Governance**: Members participate in decision-making, typically through a token-based voting system on proposals that can range from operational decisions to amendments in the DAO's code.

The costs associated with setting up a DAO include technology development, smart contract audits (to ensure security and prevent vulnerabilities), legal consultation to navigate the regulatory landscape, and community management.

Transitioning to or starting as a DAO offers several advantages, including heightened transparency, democratized decision-making, and alignment with the ethos of the blockchain community. However, it also comes with challenges like ensuring broad participation, managing diverse stakeholder interests, and addressing the legal uncertainties in various jurisdictions. As such, blockchain firms looking toward DAOs as an exit strategy must be prepared to navigate these complexities while fostering a strong, engaged community.

While DAOs offer an innovative approach to organization and governance, they also come with a unique set of challenges and potential drawbacks. The lack of a traditional hierarchical structure can lead to inefficiencies in decision-making, as consensus must be reached among a potentially large and diverse group of token holders. This process can be slow and cumbersome, particularly for urgent or complex decisions. Additionally, the democratic nature of DAOs means that decision quality is directly tied to the knowledge and engagement of the members, which can vary widely.

The risk of "mutiny," or a significant faction of members working against the interests of the DAO, is a real concern. This can manifest as voting blocs that push through decisions benefiting a minority at the expense of the larger group, or even attempts to fork the DAO, creating a parallel organization. Moreover, the reliance on smart contracts and blockchain technology means that any flaws in the code can be exploited, leading to potential loss of funds or control of the DAO.

Another significant challenge is the legal and regulatory ambiguity surrounding DAOs. Without clear legal status in many jurisdictions, members may face uncertainties regarding liability, taxation, and regulatory compliance. This ambiguity can deter potential members or investors who are concerned about the legal implications of their involvement.

These factors must be thoroughly considered and addressed by anyone looking to establish or participate in a DAO.

Chapter 11: Recommended Reading

Here are some online publications that cover blockchain technology. These sources focus on the technology, use cases, advancements, and the impact of blockchain, beyond just the financial and cryptocurrency markets. After this book it should be easy to keep up with what's going on in the space and understand the nuances of the articles. This will make your understanding more rounded and keep you up to date.

CoinDesk's Blockchain Section: While CoinDesk is primarily known for its cryptocurrency news, its Blockchain section covers a broad range of topics related to blockchain technology, including latest developments, use cases, and trends.

Cointelegraph's Blockchain Section: Similar to CoinDesk, Cointelegraph's Blockchain section provides news and analysis on the latest developments in blockchain technology.

Decrypt.co: Decrypt covers the latest news about blockchain technology and cryptocurrencies, including detailed explainers, guides, and analysis pieces.

Blockchain News: This is a dedicated site covering news, strategy, insight, and analysis around blockchain technology and its various use cases across industries. www.the-blockchain.com

The Block Crypto: The Block covers digital assets and blockchain from all angles—not only financial but technological, societal, and more. www.theblockcrypto.com

Blockchain Magazine: Blockchain Magazine covers technological developments, interviews with industry leaders, and expert insights into blockchain technology. blockchainmagazine.net

Blockonomi: Blockonomi is a fast-growing blog that covers cryptocurrencies, fintech, and the blockchain ecosystem.

101 Blockchains: This online publication offers a range of blockchain educational content, including articles, guides, webinars, and more.

CryptoSlate: While it covers crypto news, CryptoSlate also has a wide range of content focused on blockchain technology, use cases, and product launches.

Blockchain Technology News: This site provides the latest news and analysis on blockchain technology. blockchaintechnology-news.com

Blockchain Reporter.net: They focus on providing the most current blockchain news, including crypto news and fintech advancements.

Blockchain Council: The Blockchain Council creates an environment and raises awareness among businesses, enterprises, developers, and society by educating them in the blockchain space. www.blockchain-council.org

Dapp Life: They report on the latest blockchain and cryptocurrency news, including decentralized applications (Dapps), Ethereum, and more.

DappRadar Blog: This site provides updates and insights into the world of decentralized applications (Dapps) and blockchain platforms. dappradar.com/blog

Ledger Insights: Ledger Insights provides news and insights about enterprise blockchain, blockchain in business and Regtech.

Remember that the scope, focus, and direction of these publications can change over time.

Chapter 12: Conclusion

As we draw this exploration of blockchain to a close, I want to express my heartfelt gratitude to you, dear reader. It's been an enriching journey to compile, articulate, and present this compendium of knowledge, and I hope it has served as an enlightening guide in your pursuit of understanding the transformative power of blockchain technology.

The very process of writing this book has reinforced my conviction that we stand at the threshold of a new era. Blockchain, in its profound ability to redefine the boundaries of trust, transparency, and transactional integrity, has begun to etch the contours of a future that's not just promising, but also inclusive and empowering. Every page I penned was inspired by the conviction that blockchain is not just another technological innovation, but a building block and a paradigm shift.

However, as we delve into the intricacies of blockchain and envision its boundless potential, it's essential to remember that no journey worth undertaking is devoid of challenges or setbacks. The path to innovation is often uncharted and riddled with hurdles, but it's the spirit of persistence and a foundation of sound knowledge that turn these daunting adversities into stepping stones of unprecedented achievements. Don't let past failures dim your vision. It's a new space and errors will be many. We are to learn from them and walk forward on top of past mistakes.

In closing, let me reassure you that the future of blockchain is as bright as we dare to imagine. As the narrative of this revolutionary technology continues to unfold, I urge you to stay curious, keep learning, and actively participate in shaping this exciting epoch of technological evolution. For in the end, it is our collective efforts and shared vision that will determine the impact of blockchain on our lives and societies.

Here's to a future where trust is irrefutable, transactions are transparent, and innovation knows no bounds. May the knowledge gleaned from this book empower you to contribute meaningfully to the blockchain revolution and to persist in your endeavors, no matter the challenge. Remember, every great journey begins with a single step, and you've already taken that first step by arming yourself with knowledge through this book. The world of blockchain awaits your imprint. Let's venture forth into this bright future, together.

About the Author

Alex Rass is a serial entrepreneur and technology innovator with over 25 years of experience in the fintech industry, specifically in blockchain and cybersecurity. Holding senior roles in firms such as Morgan Stanley and Goldman Sachs, he has led and architected cutting-edge technological solutions. Alex's expertise extends to the development of sophisticated trading systems and pioneering blockchain applications in traditional finance and beyond.

Alex has successfully launched and led several startups, leading to multiple exits.

As a technical advisor and contributor to publications like CoinDesk and a participant in key industry forums, Alex's insights into blockchain and cybersecurity are widely recognized and sought after.

Alex developed the first-ever T0 solution for an exchange, leveraging Ethereum for transaction settlement. This innovative approach marked a significant milestone in blockchain technology. Alex also pioneered the first-to-market crypto lending business.

Alex recently developed a high-frequency trading (HFT) system for swift and efficient crypto market transactions. Additionally, he developed a specialized 'black box' system for trading cryptocurrencies and crypto options.

Through his book, Alex shares his extensive knowledge and unique perspectives on blockchain technology, aiming to illuminate its transformative potential and drive forward the digital revolution. He is a graduate of Stevens Institute of Technology with master's and bachelor's degrees in computer science.